A happy look at Aging

FACING LIFE'S CHANGES
CONFIDENTLY

A happy look at Aging

WERNER GRAENDORF

Here's Life Publishers

P.O. Box 1576, San Bernardino, CA 92402

A HAPPY LOOK AT AGING
By Werner C. Graendorf
A Campus Crusade for Christ Book

Published by
HERE'S LIFE PUBLISHERS, INC.
P.O. Box 1576
San Bernardino, Ca 92404

Library of Congress Cataloging-in Publication Data:
Graendorf, Werner C.
  A happy look at aging.
  Includes bibliographies.
    1. Aged — Conduct of life.   2. Aged — Religious life.
I. Title.
BJ1691.G73   1986   248.8'5   85-24938
ISBN 0-89840-117-8 (pbk.)
HLP Product No. 951236
© 1985, Werner C. Graendorf

Except where otherwise indicated, all Scripture quotations in this book are taken from the New American Standard Bible, © The Lockman Foundation 1960, 1962, 1963, 1968, 1971, 1972, 1973, 1975, 1977. Used by permission. Other Scripture quotations are from the *King James Version* (KJV), *The New International Version* of The Holy Bible, (NIV) © 1978 by New York International Bible Society; *The New Testament in Modern English* translated by J. B. Phillips, (Phillips) © The Macmillan Company, New York; *The Living Bible* (LB) © 1971 by Tyndale House Publishers, Wheaton, Illinois, used by permission; and the Jerusalem Bible, © 1966 Doubleday and Co., Garden City, New York.

FOR MORE INFORMATION, WRITE:

L.I.F.E. — P.O. A399, Sydney South 2000, Australia
Campus Crusade for Christ of Canada — Box 300, Vancouver, B.C., V6C 2X3, Canada
Campus Crusade for Christ — 108 Friar Street, Reading RG1 1EP, Berkshire, England
Lay Institute for Evangelism — P.O. Box 8786, Auckland 3, New Zealand
Great Commission Movement of Nigeria — P.O. Box 500, Jos, Plateau State Nigeria, West Africa
Life Ministry — P.O. Box/Bus 91015, Auckland Park 2006, Republic of South Africa
Campus Crusade for Christ International — Arrowhead Springs, San Bernardino, Ca 92414, U.S.A.

Contents

About This Book and Author

The concerned church has a challenge to provide its people opportunity for understanding (and being able to cope) through a Christian perspective on aging. Such provision, by church or individual, is a major step toward enriching older adults' quality of life.

Aging is a normal aspect of life which, fortunately, we can anticipate and prepare for. Each of us is part of the aging process. But happy is the person who understands the process well enough to make growing older a positive experience. In today's uncertain world, we need all the help we can get!

This is the purpose for *A Happy Look at Aging* — an enjoyable series of essays which provide practical guidance and encouragement to help make aging as successful as possible. In fifteen crisp, readable chapters, it touches on the major aspects of what happens as we grow older, from the physical to the social, and what to do about it.

It can also be used as a dependable text for classes and studies on the subject of older adults (a teacher/leader manual will be available). Written with an easy charm and wit, it is a book for anyone looking for some good reading on making the journey of aging more enjoyable.

The four major units, based on Jesus Christ's personal human development (noted in Luke 2:52) concern healthy aging, productive aging, confident aging, and aging that is able to cope.

Before his retirement, Werner Graendorf was chairman of the Department of Christian Education at Moody Bible Institute, Chicago, Illinois.

He received his Ph.D. from New York University and has three earned master's degrees (M.S. in Education, University of Southern California; M.R.E., Fuller Theological Seminary; M.Div., Faith Theological Seminary) and a B.A. from Wheaton College.

His background includes experience as a national boys' work executive, research director for a national teacher training program, and educational positions on both local church and state levels. He has written textbooks on Christian education and camping.

Since retiring he has done graduate work in gerontology (study of aging) at California State University/Fullerton, near the mobile home he and his wife occupy in Brea, California.

Before You Begin

We all want successful aging — to be able to make the most of each day of our life. What a great prospect!

There has been in this century a dramatic increase in the human life span. As a result, at age fifty we now have potentially twenty-five years ahead of us. Most of this would be considered older adult living, with its attendant concerns. Further, such living takes place in a steadily more complicated, constantly changing world of space exploration, computerization and economic uncertainties. We need all the encouragement we can get to help make growing older a successful, satisfying experience. It can be done!

Yet from a strictly human viewpoint, growing older is often considered a pessimistic matter of existence — to keep going until . . .! As Douglas Kimmel notes in his textbook, *Adulthood and Aging* "Aging . . . leads to a growing inability of the organism to adapt to the environment and thus to survive."[1]

But happily, there is a positive approach to aging. It is the addition of a Christian perspective — to be able to look at aging from a godly viewpoint. There's good news!

As the hymn writer Isaac Watts wrote so movingly some two hundred years ago:

> O God, our help in ages past,
> Our hope for years to come,
> Our shelter from the stormy blast,
> And our eternal home!

Here is a perspective that provides the needed guidance for effective living and growing as older adults. Yes, *growing* as older adults, for as Cardinal John Henry Newman (1801-1890) said in his autobiography, "Growth is the (only) evidence of life." So, with God's help, we will continue to grow and develop, whatever our age!

No mere existence here, but purposeful living!

But how do we grow as older adults? Again, our Christian perspective offers a practical answer, for a primary focus in Christianity, as you know, is the life as well as the work of Jesus Christ — The God-man who lived as a man for some thirty years on earth and knew what it meant to be human like us. ("The Word was God . . . the Word became flesh and lived for a while among us" (John 1:1,14 NIV).

Is there, then, indication of how Jesus developed as a person? There is, succinctly recorded in the story of His life by the physician-writer Luke: "Jesus grew in wisdom and stature, and in favor with God and men" (Luke 2:52 NIV). Most of us have applied this only to Jesus as a child. More accurately, it represents Jesus as a normal person. Thus He serves as a pattern to guide us.

Observe that this is not simply a spiritualizing approach to life. It is a practical pattern of growing that touches the major areas of normal living. Note them:

"Jesus grew . . . "

the physical   ("in stature" — *the body,* as translated by Phillips's *Modern English New Testament*)

the mental   ("in wisdom" — *the mind,* again Phillips)

the social   ("in favor with men")

the spiritual   ("in favor with God")

In their application, these four give us some basic keys for successful aging:

(a) the key of physical fitness, for *healthy* aging;

(b) the key of mental alertness, for *productive* aging;

(c) the key of social concern, for aging that is able to *cope;*

(d) the key of spiritual perspective, for *confident* aging.

The purpose of this book is to help you understand and use these keys in your own situation.

Let's face it. There is always room for improvement, to get more out of life. These pages suggest some practical ways to help do it. No book can solve all the challenges of growing older. But you will find here some good reading that will make the journey more enjoyable.

UNIT ONE

Confident Aging

UNIT ONE
Confident Aging . . .

Jesus grew . . . in favor with God (Luke 2:52, NIV).
The Lord will be your confidence (Proverbs 3:26, NASB).

How do we face aging with confidence? Happily, it can be done.

It begins with choices we need to make in determining our *attitude* about aging, just like Marge and I found ourselves making choices about the fruit on our apple tree one summer. Do we make apple pie or let the apples rot?

Next, the true heart of confident aging lies in *perspective,* the context within which we view things. Thus, while physical, mental and social concerns related to growing older are important, the path to successful aging begins with spiritual perspective — being able to see aging from God's viewpoint.

Finally, since confidence grows on facts, we also need a factual *understanding* of what aging is and, just as important, what it is not.

Here is uplifting reading, whether you are looking on your own for information and encouragement or studying with a class or discussion group.

Chapter One

ROTTING APPLES
OR APPLE PIE?

We who have made it into our second half-century have a lot going for us! Being older has increasing compensations. (J. Oswald Sanders tells us more about that in his book, *Your Best Years.*[1]) A major benefit, for instance, is the lessened pressure of time. There is often more opportunity to do the things a ticking clock once limited.

Consider hobbies and recreation. Many of us can look forward to travel and reading. But there is also the challenging possibility of more time for such things as personal Bible study, intercessory prayer, and a vast array of practical church and community service projects. The biblical writer Paul encourages "making the most of your time" (Ephesians 5:16).

There are a substantial number of older adults. For example, there are now more than 25,000,000 retired Americans,[2] or 66 percent more than when social security was initiated in 1935. Politicians and the media already have realized we have a significant influence socially, as well as economically and politically. The older adult in America today is important.

We've seen intriguing life-span changes. At the beginning of this century the expected length of life in America was an average of forty-seven years. Today it is closer to seventy-five!

However, the idea of extended years in today's world doesn't particularly impress one of my neighbors. "What's so great about living longer?" he notes pessimistically. "Have you read the morning newspaper?" He may have a point.

But wait a minute. Life for older adults is a good deal like having an apple tree in your back yard. You can, as we found out one summer, ignore the apples and let them pile up to rot. Makes a mess. Or you can make apple pie, as we did the next summer. Much better.

Some older adults let life spoil on them as they do little with it except bemoan inconveniences. Others, with a bit of effort, "make apple pie"; they use their available time and energy to be productive and fulfilled, and in the process make life worth living.

This is what Dangott and Kalish, authorities in the field of aging, are getting at, I believe, when they write, "Aging . . . is a style of living that we create."[3]

We can do much to *make* life worthwhile. A good example is Caleb in the Bible. Part of the Joshua-Caleb minority team that brought back a positive report on that famous survey of the Promised Land, Caleb kept a positive outlook throughout his life. Thus, rather than giving in to normal decline of age, he accepted the challenge of a new venture when the land was being divided (see Joshua 14). "With the Lord's help," the second oldest man in the Israelite nation told Joshua, "for my assignment, I'd like to tackle the rugged hill country!"

God can give each of us Caleb-like courage for living as older adults.

It is well to remind ourselves that to a large extent our experience is guided by what we are looking for in that experience. It's somewhat like the two sisters taking a walk after a rainstorm. One complained bitterly about the mud puddles in the path. The other sister avoided the mud puddles but spoke cheerily about the violets along the path that would be blooming soon because of the rain. You know who enjoyed the walk.

We have some good friends in our mobile home park who share with us in the aging experience, and we delight to be with them, whether for lunch or just a casual dish of ice cream at the end of the day. Recently it struck us that while there is more than a decade of age difference between us, it is a completely negligible factor in our easy relationship.

The reason, I think, reflects a steadiness that comes from the simple faith in God that characterizes George and Agnes. They are a couple who have maintained a positive approach to living, and not only has it kept zest in their own lives, but it also has made them good company for those who associate with them.

Make no mistake, getting older is not always a hilarious experience. As an older friend said when she heard about the book on aging, *The Joy of Growing Older,*[4] "Joy in aging? Tell it to my aching back!"

Yet keep in mind that, regardless of aging circumstances, whether you see mud puddles or violets along the path is still largely your decision! Your later years can be kept, if you will, like that fresh-baked apple pie — full of zestful flavor.

Remember, too, that successful aging is a partnership — a partnership of determination (yours) and strength (Christ's).

I have always enjoyed Edgar Guest's little ditty on determination:

> Somebody said that it couldn't be done,
>   But he with a chuckle replied
> That "maybe it couldn't," but he would be one
>   Who wouldn't say so till he'd tried.
>
> So he buckled right in with the trace of a grin
>   On his face. If he worried he hid it.
> He started to sing as he tackled the thing
>   That couldn't be done, and he did it.[5]

But I also recognize the resources that need to go with that determination: "I can do all things through Christ which strengtheneth me" (Philippians 4:13, KJV). Here is the essential factor of the Christian perspective, Christ living in us and expressing Himself through the power of the Holy Spirit. In this way we can indeed face aging with a happy outlook.

Suggestions for Enriching Your Study

Realize that effective aging begins and continues with your own determination to do something about it. And success is a partnership that draws on God's strength for accomplishment.

(a) Meditate on and possibly discuss with someone else the implications of *partnership* for effective aging. Note the example of David in the battle with Goliath — David's determination (1 Samuel 17:32, 40, 49) and God's strength (1 Samuel 17:37, 45, 47).

(b) Consider what led aging Caleb to ask Joshua for the rugged hill country as his land allotment (Joshua 14:10-12).

(c) Write out three objectives for yourself on what you would like to gain from this study on aging (for example, to develop a personal exercise program).

Chapter Two

DON'T FORGET THE CINNAMON!

Mother was an old fashioned German cook. Consequently, the delightful aroma and taste of freshly baked goodies such as *streussel* and *pflaumen kuchen* are a happy part of my childhood memories.

However, despite the old country specialties, the overall family baking favorite remained crisp apple pie. There was something about the way Mom put the ingredients together that produced apple pie whose flavor had no competition. It never failed — except that day the relatives came from Chicago for Sunday dinner. Actually, as I remember, the dinner itself went well, right up to the dessert. But for once the famous apple pie was below par.

The story came out after the guests had left. Mother, seemingly unflustered by the challenge of a house full of critical relatives, had nevertheless succumbed to the pressure during the preparation of the pie. She somehow left out the crucial ingredient — her special cinnamon spice mix. It made all the difference.

So that day, the remembrance of an uncharacteristicly flavorless apple pie became indelibly embedded in our minds, originating the family expression that when anything was below par, the "cinnamon" had been left out.

It may be that the cinnamon has been left out of your life as an older adult. Perhaps we can help you restore it, for we're talking about the flavor of a Christian perspective — being able to look at aging from God's viewpoint. It makes all the difference.[1]

In the perspective of God as creator, the Christian believer recognizes that he is a God-created being and that regardless of age or appearance, he is significant. "God created man in His own image . . . male and female He created them" (Genesis 1:27). "It is he who made us, and we are his" (Psalm 100:3, NIV).

Our personal value relates to our position as a member of God's family; it does not change just because we are aging. "To all who received him, to those who believed in his name, he gave the right to become children of God" (John 1:12, NIV).

Happy is the individual of any age who has established a relationship with God that enables him to come to God as to a Father. This is accomplished by the simple step of accepting God's forgiveness for his sins, provided through the death and resurrection of Jesus Christ.

This means I apply John 3:16 to my life by telling God so. ("For God so loved the world, that he gave his only begotten Son, that whosoever believeth in him should not perish, but have everlasting life", KJV). ("Thank you, God, for loving me. I believe that Jesus died for my sins and that through Him I now have eternal life.")[2]

The Christian also realizes that God is the supreme architect. " . . . whose architect and builder is God" (Hebrews 11:10). Just as Abraham had this perspective for all of life, so we can recognize God as the divine planner who guides the destiny of all lives, including ours. Whether sixteen or sixty, I am part of a master plan: I am here for a purpose. ". . . having been chosen beforehand in accordance with the intent of Him whose might carries out in everything the design of his own will." (Ephesians 1:11, Weymouth).

Thank God, there is a meaningful plan and purpose for my life as an older adult!

Finally, the Christian perspective adds the ongoing zest of God as sustainer. We are reminded again of the testimony of eighty-five-year-old Caleb, about the Lord's keeping him strong and well (Joshua 14:10,11).

God not only created me for a purpose but He provides for me until that purpose is completed. An old preacher friend once told me during a death-fearing stage in my life, "You are immortal until your life's work is done."

The sustaining care of God for His people is expressed pithily in David's words in Psalm 55:22 (NIV), "Cast your cares on the Lord and he will sustain you."

Whatever our age, we have a heavenly Father who watches over us. The story of the boat captain's son expresses it well. One day when the boy was on his father's sightseeing boat, a sudden, severe storm came up and some of the passengers became panicky. Seeing their concern, the boy felt the need to reassure the passengers.

"Not to worry," he calmly told them. "My father is the captain, and he knows how to take care of storms!"

Some years ago William Ernest Henley wrote the well-known poem "Invictus" on the theme of a man's control over his own destiny. Later, Dorothea Day wrote a response entitled "My Captain" that pictures well the role of God as sustainer. Note the comparison:

INVICTUS

Out of the night that covers me,
Black as the pit from pole to pole,
I thank whatever gods may be
For my unconquerable soul.

In the fell clutch of circumstance
I have not winced nor cried aloud.
Under the bludgeonings of chance
My head is bloody, but unbowed.

Beyond this place of wrath and tears
Looms but the horror of the shade,
And yet the menace of the years
Finds, and shall find, me unafraid.

It matters not how strait the gate,
How charged with punishments the scroll,
I am the master of my fate:
I am the captain of my soul.

William Ernest Henley[2]

Clearly, the Christian perspective on aging contains more than a future hope (although that future hope is an exciting part of the Christian perspective and the theme of one of the final chapters).

Being able to look at aging from God's view with its ongoing implications of God as creator, architect and sustainer is a present encouragement for each of us as we face the vicissitudes of life. Christ is indeed Captain, here and now!

So hear again the assuring words of the psalmist David,:

"I was young and now I am old, yet I have never seen the righteous forsaken" (Psalm 37:25, NIV).

MY CAPTAIN

Out of the light that dazzles me,
Bright as the sun from pole to pole,
I thank the God I know to be
For Christ the conqueror of my soul.

Since His the sway of circumstances
I would not wince nor cry aloud.
Under that rule which men call chance
My head with joy is humbly bowed.

Beyond this place of sin and tears
That life with Him! And His the aid,
Despite the menace of the years,
Keeps, and shall keep me, unafraid.

I have no fear, though strait the gate,
He cleared from punishment the scroll.
Christ is the Master of my fate.
Christ is the Captain of my soul.

Dorothea Day[3]

Suggestions for Enriching Your Study

Note the calming, encouraging effect that a Christian perspective (approach) can make on the subject of aging.

(a) What does it mean to "leave out the cinnamon"?

(b) Using a concordance, study other words that help explain God as sustainer, God as architect, or God as creator for the older adult.

(c) Which of the three perspectives — creator, architect, or sustainer — is most significant for you? Why?

Chapter Three

UNDERSTANDING AGING

Aging is when you walk with your head held high — trying to get used to your tri-focals.

What happens to us as we grow older? What can we do about it?

Aging is a perfectly natural process. But so often we allow misconceptions (aging myths) to diminish what otherwise could be a satisfying, productive time of life.

Perhaps my childhood Frogtown schoolhouse experience will illustrate.

I grew up on the edge of what many considered a midwestern ghost town. At one time the town thrived because of a piano factory, which eventually closed, leaving a scattering of deserted buildings, including a fire-scarred schoolhouse.

The town drew its local name of Frogtown from a low area that during the spring rainy season became an isolated swamp teeming with frogs. I remember sitting on our front porch on quiet summer evenings, listening to the distant croaking from the swamp.

As you might imagine, the area was a young boy's dream come true. Besides the swamp full of frogs, the deserted buildings provided unlimited exploration adventure. What great fun we had as we clambered in and out of those decrepit buildings, gleefully chasing whatever wildlife occupied the weed-covered premises!

But the fun ceased abruptly one June night.

Because some of the older boys in the area didn't like the younger kids playing in "their" territory, especially in the "dangerous" old schoolhouse, they told us that some years past, before the school was officially closed, there had been a bad fire in it. Some of the kids still attending then had been badly burned, and a few had died. Now, the story developed, those dead students came back regularly to guard the premises, and we were warned that it was dangerous to be caught in there at any time. If we doubted any of this, the older boys suggested that we go over with them some night and find out for ourselves!

I don't remember all the details, but one night several of us did manage to sneak over to the old schoolhouse accompanied by some of the older fellows. Sure enough, as we younger boys shakily felt our way into the schoolhouse shell that night, we heard some eerie fluttering noises and weird commotion.

None of us (I think) believed there were actually any dead kids running around, as the older fellows had warned us. But at the age of eight, in a deserted building at night, you don't take any chances. As a result, that night marked the end of our Frogtown exploration fun.

As I look back, I suppose we should have talked with our parents about those stories the older guys told us, but so far as I know, no one ever did. We just gave up our fun.

As a matter of fact, the fire in the schoolhouse had actually been caused by the older boys themselves when they used the building as a hideout for smoking. The fluttering commotion so frightening that night came from bats.

The Frogtown schoolhouse experience, in retrospect, shows how accepting uncertain information can result in misconceptions. This certainly applies to aging. Through the lack of accurate information and acceptance of aging caricatures, many persons unfortunately perceive growing older as a miserable condition. So you might hear, for example, that an older person is one who spends much time in the hospital.

Not true, says aging expert, K. Warner Schaie. He points out:

> In any given year, around 83 percent of the elderly do *not* require short-term hospital care, and only 9 percent of a surveyed elderly group rated their health as poor.[1]

Schaie goes on to list some forty other possible myths (misconceptions).

The pioneering work in the correction of misunderstandings about aging has been done by Robert Butler in *Why Survive?*, his Pulitzer Prize winning study on aging. He notes such erroneous concerns as senility, inflexibility and unproductivity, which we will touch on in later chapters.

Dr. Butler, the first director of the National Institute on Aging, points out in the first chapter of his book, "Old age is neither inherently miserable nor inherently sublime — like every stage of life it has problems, joys, fears and potentials."[2]

Our concern, then, is not to ignore the realities of aging, but rather to make certain that they are realities, not the mistaken ideas referred to by Sanders in *Your Best Years* as "predatory myths that need to be frightened away."[3]

How, then, do we understand aging?

There are plenty of humorous notes on aging. (Serious disabilities of aging are, of course, no laughing matter, and it is important to avoid humor that demeans or is offensive. Yet there is a legitimate place for looking at the lighter side.)

Tilman Smith has a fine chapter on humor called "Beyond Tiddleywinks: Exercise and Humor" in his book, *In Favor of Growing Older:*

> In order that our days may be both long and fruitful on this earth we should have a sense of humor. Nearly all longevity studies have found this to be an important ingredient. To have a sense of humor does not mean that we become trite, fickle, silly, or irresponsible. It means rather that we do not take ourselves too seriously, our personal dignity can stand some adjusting, and we can actually learn to enjoy a situation where "the joke is on us." Humor can relieve tensions and keep us from becoming too rigid . . . a tonic for the soul . . .[4]

I like that, and find a hearty chuckle in such items as the definition of aging that suggests it is the stage of life when you sit in a rocking chair — but can't get it going!

More scientifically, Jon Hendricks and C. Davis Hendricks in *Aging in Mass Society,* suggest that growing older is a process involving various bodily changes.[5] Another standard text, Douglas Kimmel's *Adulthood and Aging,* emphasizes decline in physical competence.[6]

What these definitions are saying is that as we grow older there are changes in our physical, mental and social abilities. Most of us over the age of fifty have become aware of this.

For women there are such considerations as the menopause. For men it can mean such things as learning to tackle teen-age sons (both literally and figuratively) with caution!

Helen Hayes, the indomitable first lady of the American theatre, has in *Our Best Years,* her delightful book of reminiscences (written when she was 83), an essay titled "Psychoneuroimmunology." Aside from being difficult to pronounce (she confesses it took her a day of practice), the essay reminds us of the place of good mental attitude in older adult health.

Her conclusion is worth quoting: "Positive attitudes — optimism, high self-esteem, an outgoing nature, joyousness, and the ability to cope with stress — when established early in life, may be the most important basis for continued good health."[7]

As we grow older, keeping a positive attitude becomes an increasing challenge. Often the slowing down of abilities or energies leads to subtle self-pity, giving a negative cast to life. For some, especially those with strongly structured work tendencies, retirement, with its relaxing of schedules and responsibilities, can create such a negative attitude. Don't let it happen to you!

Two suggestions. First, many of us have found a "picker-upper" helpful — something that enables us to readjust our perspective.

I think of Sam Levenson as such a pick-up. Sam was part of an East Harlem family, and through his writing and television programs in the mid-60s he adroitly described what it was like growing up with six brothers and a sister in a New York tenement. He describes his neighborhood, for instance, as a metropolitan section that the sight-seeing guides called a slum and the sociologists identified as a depressed area. "Yet," he writes in *Everything But Money,* "I never felt depressed or deprived. My environment was miserable; I was not. . . . Poverty never succeeded in degrading our family. We were independently poor."[8]

Here is a positive approach to living!

"I went on my merry way being merry simply because I did not know any better," writes Sam. "I didn't know,

for instance, . . . I needed some quiet place where I
could do my homework. My brothers used to sit around
the dining room table in the evening doing homework
en masse, noisily, bothering each other. . . . They didn't
know they were doing it all wrong. Tough luck! It's too
late to rectify it now that they are educated and doing
nicely."[9]

"As an additional safeguard against self-pity in our
home," he adds, "Mamma kept several charity boxes
marked 'For the Poor.' We gave to the poor regularly. It
made us feel rich."[10]

Along the way, one of the Levensons became a doctor
(Fordham University). Among the delightful episodes in
Sam's portrayal of Levenson family life is the story of
the day the medical student brought home the model
skull.

"The brothers," Sam relates, "placed it in the bookcase. At night they would put a lighted candle into it to
scare off burglars."

"It worked," he reports. "The one burglar who got
in was so terrified he forgot his tools!"[11]

My dad had his own special perspective readjuster.
"Mutter," he would say in his German accent, "I think
it is time for some ice cream."

Mom, on the other hand, would do her readjusting
by taking out her knitting needles and tackling another
sweater. I still have a number of lovely samples of her
work.

So we each have our way of adjusting perspective.
For one person it may be collecting stamps (which my
uncle always insisted was a foolish hobby, especially if
the stamps were used; he encouraged his nephew to
collect gold coins). Another person finds photography
does it for him. The point is to have something that
absorbs your interest enough to allow you to shift your

focus. (For suggestions, see Chapter 7, "No Time for Rusting.")

A second help for keeping a fresh approach to living is learning to balance the negatives with pluses.

I go back to the two sisters and the rainstorm (the illustration used previously). What a happy facility it is to see violets despite mud puddles!

Remember the classic story of the lad whose thoughtful grandfather gave him two half dollars one hot July day to purchase ice cream sundaes for himself and his little sister? On the way to the ice cream shop one of the half dollars somehow slipped out of his pocket and rolled into a gopher hole.

"How fortunate it was," the boy reported later on a positive note to his grandfather, "that although we lost sister's half dollar, I was able to hold on to mine!"

Seriously, as we consider aging and its physical changes, it is well to remind ourselves of what truly extraordinary machines our human bodies are. Alexis Carrel, the Nobel Prize winning French surgeon, provides some dramatic insight into just how remarkable in his best-selling *Man the Unknown:*

> The body is extremely robust. It adapts itself to all climates — Arctic cold as well as tropical heat. It also resists starvation, weather inclemencies, fatigue, hardships. Man is the hardiest of all animals. We always unconsciously compare the body with a machine . . . but the endurance of man comes from the elasticity of the tissue, their tenacity, their property of growing instead of wearing out; from their strange power of adaptive change. Resistance to disease, work and worries, capacity for effort, and nervous equilibrium are the signs of the superiority of a man.[12]

Few, if any, man-built machines can compete with what the human body is able to accomplish day after day, often under conditions of severe stress and misuse. This is well illustrated in the aging process.

The body continually makes remarkable adjustments for age. It has the ability to compensate for injuries and weaknesses in almost every part. So, while physical changes are one of the marks of growing older, still the creator has provided us with physical equipment that, with reasonable care, provides us with truly amazing service!

The physician, Alfred Heller, in his book on physical fitness speaks of the "wonder of our temple of clay"[13] as he reminds us of Psalm 139:13,14: "You created my inmost being; you knit me together in my mother's womb . . . I am fearfully and wonderfully made" (NIV).

Let's note briefly some of the physical adjustments of this "temple of clay."

By age fifty, most people have had to correct changes in their vision by using eye glasses or contact lenses. The lenses of our eyes have become harder and less flexible, with resulting farsightedness from the reduced elasticity. Eye difficulty after the age of fifty often relates to night driving, where the problem of adjusting from glare (headlights) to dimness (dark roadways and surrounding areas) creates driving tension. Many older adults prefer to avoid night driving when possible.

Eye cataracts (the clouding of the eye lens) often must be treated. However, they are no longer the consuming difficulty they were in the past, as modern eye care now offers relatively simple operations that can restore nearly normal vision.

And though the other major physical adjustment concerns hearing, it also has been relieved greatly by modern medical advances. Hearing aids today show major improvements in both size and effectiveness.

One of the most common (Arthritis Foundation figures indicate that there are some 35,000,000 people affected) chronic difficulties of the elderly is arthritis (inflamation of the joints). The two most common forms are osteo (breakdown of bone structure in the lower back and in joints) and rheumatoid (more in the smaller joints).

Along with the traditional aspirin and heat treatment, there is a growing emphasis on supervised exercise. Thus, organizations such as the Arthritis Foundation encourage the use of such materials as Buster Crabbe's *Arthritis Exercise Book*[14] in recommended exercise programs.

The physical aspect of aging also includes arteriosclerosis (hardening of the arteries) and atherosclerosis (cholesterol buildup which causes coronary artery disease).

There is increased understanding of what happens to the body physically in aging. For example, a study is being done on collagen (the fibrous protein which serves as the body's connective tissue, whose loss of plastic properties causes such problems as skin wrinkling) which has challenging possibilities for lessening deterioration.

There are positive factors in the mental aspects of aging, too. First, there is the matter of older adult *learning.* What can the aging adult expect to do mentally? How practical is adult education for the over-fifty person? A summary in Schaie gives this challenging picture:

> If you keep your health and engage your mind with the problems and activities of the world around you, chances are good that you will experience little if any decline in intellectual performance in your lifetime. That's the promise of research in the area of adult intelligence.[15]

A related consideration is *memory.* Here again, on the basis of a wide range of studies, the word is encouraging:

> . . . very little decline in the ability to learn and remember until very late in life. . . Motivation is perhaps the key variable in adult education . . . for old dogs rarely have difficulty *learning* new tricks; they more often have diffi-

culty convincing themselves that a bone is worth the effort.[16]

The social aspects of aging concern changing relationships with people — family, friends, neighbors, sexual partner. Some of this is outside the older person's control because of society's attitude toward the aging, such as the sterotyping noted before; e.g., older as sickly. The older person can either encourage such stereotypes by his own negative attitude and actions or he can demonstrate a positiveness which will help disprove the "myth" and project an optimistic picture.

A primary area of social involvement is family, and one of the big challenges in aging is the relationship with one's children — the ability to continue mutually enjoyable contact and activity with them. This means, of course, to recognize the variances in interests and responsibilities that come with aging for both parents and children.

There are other major social concerns. Along with the increased life span there is increased concern for the care of aging parents. There is also the retirement factor, as for many persons retirement represents severing basic social ties.

Richard Kalish summarizes the people aspect of growing older on a positive note as he comments that the social relationships:

> . . . are the source of many of life's most exciting, pleasurable, and satisfying moments . . . many elderly people maintaining rich relationships with family members, friends, and more casual acquaintances throughout their lives.[17]

We can define growing older, then, from the perspective of adjustment — changes in our physical, mental, and social abilities and interests. Like all adjustments, these require effort. But the encouraging note is that in a majority of cases there are positive results. Our eyes adjust satisfactorily to glasses, we write notes rather than depend solely on memory, we learn to tolerate aches, and the grandchildren are happy to come visit. We adjust pretty well!

But there is another familiar way of defining aging, namely in terms of checking off birthdays. This is chronological definition. We all remember the eagerly awaited sweet sixteen of driver's license significance. Yet this sometimes seems to be quickly followed by Jack Benny's "thirty-nine and holding" perspective.

Especially significant in chronology is the social security retirement age of sixty-five (sixty-two for early retirement) which for most Americans has become the pivotal mark in aging.

Although convenient, birthdays as an aging guide are a relatively poor measure of the aging process, for age significance is steadily changing. Witness the gradual elimination of mandatory age sixty-five retirement, the increasing emphasis on adult education, and the expanding recognition of the positive place of the older citizen in today's society. All this is combining to steadily erode the chronologically-oriented stereotype of the "aging" adult.

Actually, behavior and self-concept are becoming more accepted measures for aging. The person who once was expected to find a corner and quietly rock his over-sixty years away now runs for (and wins) the presidency of his country.

The steady change in the expected image of the older person is significantly reflected in the shift in language used to identify him. Butler speaks pertinently to this as he writes:

> Perhaps even a new name is in order. All our terms for old age conjure up negative images — some more, some less. Few people are willing to be identified as "aged," "aging," "elderly," "old-timer," "gramps," "granny," or

even "old" itself. "Senior citizens" or "golden-ager" are
sugary euphemisms. "Old fogy," "old biddy," "old gal,"
"crock" and "geezer" are putdowns. We can either rehabili-
tate the least objectionable of these names (perhaps "elderly" and "old") to a new and respected status, or we
can come up with a new name altogether.[18]

As you'll note, we have used the term *older adult.*
While there is no established age bracket for this designa-
tion, a general consensus would begin it in the sixties.
The *middle adult* would be thirty-five to sixty-four, and
the *young adult* period is eighteen to thirty-four.

Perhaps the most typical description of today's older
adult is that we are changing. It has, in effect, really
become a different ball game. A dramatic illustration can
be found in the story of the "subway granny."

While Marge and I were living in New York City
some years ago, there was an extensive rash of subway
muggings. Despite increased police patrol on the sub-
ways, it became a constant hazard to ride anywhere at
night, especially for an older woman.

The news media then reported the story of a grand-
motherly-looking lady who was riding a subway train
one night when a gang of three young toughs invaded
the car she was sitting in. They proceeded to harass the
passengers for jewelry and money, demanding it be put
into the hat one of the gang held out.

Seeing the elderly lady sitting by herself, one of the
toughs yelled over, "You, too, granny!"

Now there might have been a time when an older
woman by herself at night would have naturally and
meekly taken off her earrings and emptied her purse
into the hat.

But this is a new day for older adults, and evidently
the way the young fellow said "granny" hit her mad
button. Swinging her good-sized purse as an attack

weapon, she moved in on the gang screaming, "Who do you think you're calling 'granny'?"

According to the news story, this ungranny-like behavior caught the three so completely by surprise that there was thorough panic as they fell over themselves trying to escape the swinging purse. In the process several of the other passengers took up the attack and succeeded in pinning the ruffians down for the security guards.

The report further indicated that by the time the guards got there, there were some very subdued toughs, including one with a broken arm. The broken arm, incidentally, was courtesy of the "granny" who, besides being in tip-top physical shape from regular attendance at a health club, had also become an expert in karate, taught as protection for "weak" elderly women.

The ultimate point, I guess, is always to smile when you call someone "granny." Aging isn't what it used to be!

Suggestions for Enriching Your Study

Seek a practical understanding of what is involved in becoming older.

(a) What is an aging myth that has hampered you from enjoying getting older?

(b) What physical adjustment have you personally made in aging?

UNIT TWO

Healthy Aging

UNIT TWO
Healthy Aging . . .

Jesus grew . . . in stature (Luke 2:52, NIV).
Be in good health (3 John 2).

The process of aging, whatever your particular situation may be, takes place in a very human body. As with anything human, that involves maintenance.

We are talking about keeping healthy as older adults, maintaining a reasonably well body. Fortunately, with a little effort, most of us can manage it.

As an aspiring fisherman, I've enjoyed the writing of Izaak Walton, who in his renowned *Compleat Angler* dispenses both piscatorial and general wisdom. Writing some 300 years ago, Walton astutely observed that "health is . . . a blessing that money cannot buy . . . if you have it, praise God, and value it."[1] Well said, Izaak Walton!

But what do we mean by health? During the national emphasis on health in the '60s, the term physical fitness became popularized. It was defined then in government publications as body strength, stamina and flexibility — basically, the ability to be an active person.[2]

(Significantly, fitness is the term used by some Bible translators, such as Phillips in the *Modern English New Testament,* for exercise in 1 Timothy 4:8.)

Secretary of Health and Human Services, Margaret M. Heckler, made clear her feelings as health secretary on the importance of fitness:

More than any other single factor, fitness determines the quality of our lives — whether we're healthy or sick, whether we can do more, live longer, feel better tomorrow than we do today.[3]

But how do we develop and maintain fitness? *The American Medical Association Family Medical Guide* has suggested three broad guidepoints for healthy living (fitness):

  (a) avoiding harmful intake, such as smoking and immoderate drinking;
  (b) regular exercise;
  (c) proper nutrition, i.e., balanced diet and avoidance of overweight.[4]

The first chapter in this unit, then, discusses the matter of keeping in as good physical condition as possible by using *exercises* that are within our interest and ability.

The second chapter looks at *nutrition* and the key contribution proper diet makes to effective living for older adults.

The third chapter assumes that a Christian perspective on growing older does not eliminate comfort as it considers *living arrangements* pointed toward moderate means.

The concluding chapter considers zestful *activity*. Being healthy is not only a matter of avoiding sickness. As defined by the World Health Organization, health is "a complete state of well-being." That means, among other things, keeping active enough to maintain interest and challenge in life.

Chapter Four

KEEP THE MACHINERY GOING!

Arnold Palmer is a world-renowned golfer. Perhaps you've seen his television commercial for motor oil. It shows Palmer in running togs, coming back from a workout; he introduces the motor oil with the suggestion that "you've got to keep the old machinery going!"

Keeping fit is one of the basic challenges of life. Like any machine, the human body needs movement to keep in condition. That means exercise — planned bodily movement to develop and maintain physical fitness. That subject gets a variety of reactions.

There are the fitness enthusiasts who insist that their personal schedule of pushups and pulls has the machine going at least an extra ten years.

On the other hand, there are the Wilbur Smith type of exercise devotees. Legend has it that the renowned Bible teacher once explained to his seminary students that when he got the urge to exercise he would lie down until the feeling went away!

Seriously, what is the place of exercise for older adults? In a day of steadily increasing interest in physical fitness (one estimate claims twenty-five million daily joggers), how important is it to have some kind of exercise program? Can exercising actually make life more liveable, or even prolong it?

There are some important factors for us to consider.

To begin with, we need to remember that although we are living in a day of unprecedented conveniences, these are conveniences that often not only provide easier living but also deprive us of natural opportunities for physical movement.

The Reader's Digest guide on health, *Eat Better, Live Better,* explains it dramatically:

> A host of modern conveniences deprive us of natural opportunities to use our bodies. We prefer vacuum cleaners to brooms and mops, elevators and escalators to stairs, golf carts to legs, snow blowers to snow shovels. Gas, electric, and oil heat has eliminated the need to chop wood or shovel coal, and today we needn't even exert ourselves by walking across the room to switch channels on the TV set — we can do it by remote control. As a result, we just don't burn up enough calories. Instead, we get fat, flabby, and weak.[1]

As one writer has put it, we have become "the victims of good living." We all probably can give stories to illustrate.

I remember well my own experience. Sitting in the family car one day, waiting patiently to restart the engine I had just stalled, I suddenly realized what I was doing. Here I sat, trying to get the car started so I could drive a letter I had just completed to the corner mail box — one short half block down the street! I might have felt even more chagrined if one of my neighbors, when I told him my experience, hadn't admitted doing the same thing!

Charles Kuntzleman, in the book, *Rating the Exercises,* has this rather incriminating comment, "Our sedentary life-style has contributed to a host of ailments that affect our health, vitality, vigor, and productivity."[2]

The need for exercise certainly seems clear. Fortunately, as a nation, we are becoming more aware of its importance, as newer medical guides indicate. We have in our home two such medical guides. A 1973 edition refers casually to exercise, mainly in reference to concerns like arthritis and general easing of stiffness. But our family medical guide begins with basic rules for healthy living, of which the central item is exercise!

Two main benefit areas are considered. The first relates to physical benefits such as strength and resiliency for heart and lungs. As the AMA Family Medical Guide observes:

> During physical exercise, you must breathe more deeply to get more oxygen into your lungs, and your heart . . . must beat harder and faster to pump blood to the muscles. Heart disease accounts for almost a third of all deaths and a high proportion of serious illness in North America. So an efficient, resilient heart, not to mention strong lungs, means you are less likely to have major health problems compared to a non-exercising contemporary.[3]

Besides the physical, there are psychological benefits, as the AMA Guide again spells out: "Many people sleep better after exercise, wake up more refreshed, and are more alert and better able to concentrate."[4]

An interesting note relating to exercise benefits is emphasized by Herbert deVries, the author of *Fitness After 50.* He refers to the "tranquilizer effect" of exercise. Noting that Americans spend more than $300 million each year on tranquilizers and sedatives, deVries, who is director of the physiology of exercise laboratory at the University of Southern California, observes that experiments indicate that regular exercise can indeed help relax a tense body and a stressed mind.[5]

Jane Brody, personal health columnist for the New York Times, notes similarly in her book on personal health that exercise tends to relieve anxiety and tension. In the same context, she comments that a practical benefit of exercise is the substantial reduction of medical bills.[6]

Finally, the Reader's Digest guide on good health adds this specifically for the older adult:

> Many researchers are sure that regular exercise slows most symptoms of aging such as fat accumulation, weakened muscles, and reduced balance, flexibility, agility, and reaction time.[7]

In the same vein, Magda Rosenberg points out in *Sixty-Plus and Fit Again* that "stiffness and decreased mobility of joints are too readily attributed to 'age' or 'arthritis,' when in fact it is poor conditioning, which is often promptly reversed by exercise."[8]

And Dr. David Stonecypher cites his simple Law of Aging: "If an individual wishes to remain vigorous, he must keep his body exercised."[9]

Summing up the whole matter, the AMA medical guide expresses clearly that "exercise of the right type should made you feel better, look better, live longer and have less illness."[10] What great incentive for giving serious consideration to some type of exercise!

The preliminary step is to recognize that since we are all individuals, we need to find activity with which we are personally comfortable. It must be something we are able and willing to take on consistently. Notice, please, that we are not talking here about participating in a sports program. Our concern is for physical fitness, defined by the Reader's Digest guide on health as "the ability to move freely and energetically."[11]

There are various exercise possibilities. In our mobile home park we have a fine tennis court, and each day there is an exuberant group of older enthusiasts enjoying the challenge of several sets of their favorite sport. (Importantly, they maintain their good physical condition with adequate warmups as part of the activity.)

But another neighbor thinks the "old duffers" are demented to be working that hard on the tennis court. He enjoys a nice, easy thirty minutes of laps in the swimming pool. On the other hand, my Marge has a TV calisthenics program which does it for her.

There are at least three major categories of exercise. The ongoing takes advantage of normal activities such as walking. Sports uses the competitive spirit of such activities as bowling and tennis. Calisthenics help provide the pushes and stretches to keep the "machine" limbered up. The essential factor is to have an activity about which you are motivated enough to keep at it. Often a key can be doing it with others.

While there is no one "best" exercise, surveys show the most popular activities to be walking, bowling, bicycling, swimming, calisthenics, golf, softball and jogging, somewhat in that order.[12]

The top-rated activity is walking as a planned exercise. It has a lot going for it. Primary for our interest is that it has no age limitations. Edward Payson Weston, known as the father of American walking, walked from New York City to Minneapolis at the age of seventy-four. That's walking!

Walking requires no special training or equipment beyond comfortable walking shoes. It has no seasonal limits and can be done in almost any area. All in all, walking undoubtedly provides one of the most practical opportunities available for developing and maintaining fitness. (It is inspiring to see neighbors like Norma Zimmer walking regularly.)

But does it actually do all that much good just to take a walk? Well, listen to what Doctor Albert Marchetti presents in his *Walking Book.* "Walking is the most efficient exercise for man . . . as a true aerobic exercise, it is just as effective in promoting fitness as running, jogging, swimming, or cycling."[13] Take heart, all you nonathletic types!

To help you get the most benefit out of your walking, the President's Council on Physical Fitness has made these suggestions: Walk tall, keep head and chest high; swing legs directly forward from hip joints; push feet off the ground — don't shuffle; swing shoulders and arms freely and easily; take deep breaths.[14]

Good walking pace is about three miles per hour. Try a brisk thirty-five minutes before or after meals.

To make walking an ultimately effective exercise, add aerobics. Now considered the world's most popular fitness program, the concept of aerobic exercise was popularized by the research and writing of Dr. Kenneth Cooper in the late '60s.

Essentially the concept refers to "a variety of exercises that stimulate heart and lung activity for time periods sufficiently long to produce beneficial changes in the body."[15]

Cooper himself points out the purpose of this type of exercise to be "increasing the amount of oxygen consumption, as measured by the pulse (heart beat)."[16]

There is a simple explanation of aerobic walking, with an age-coded heart rate chart, in the June 1984 *Reader's Digest,* pp. 141-146. A complete program of aerobics is in Cooper's *New Aerobics.*

By way of summary, physical exercise can be a vital factor in the quality of your life as an older person. The kind of exercise to use can range from active sports through calisthenics, and includes ongoing activity such as walking.

Whatever the activity is, there are some general guidelines:

(a) Do something.

(b) Do something regularly (most experts recommend a minimum of three times weekly).

(c) Choose exercise that fits your abilities and interests (enjoy it; don't overdo).

(d) Keep in mind aerobic factors for ultimate value (working toward measureable heart and lung action).

(e) Use warm-up/stretching to prepare the body for exercising; use cooling down at the end of the activity; in all excercises, go slowly.

Anderson's *Stretching* book provides basic stretching guidance for various types of exercises, e.g., hiking, running, gymnastics, golf, volleyball, walking. The basic purpose in stretching is slowly and smoothly to reduce muscle tension, help coordination, promote circulation. Essentially, stretching "provides a link between the sedentary life and the active life".[17]

(f) Keep motivated. The *Reader's Digest* health guide expresses it well: "Whichever activity you choose, the hardest exercise is the first move — beginning a physical fitness program."[18] (For further suggestions on motivation, see chapter 9.)

The Christian's perspective on exercise finds focus in such biblical references as 1 Corinthians 6:19,20: ". . . do you not know that your body is a temple of the Holy Spirit . . . you are not your own? For you have been bought with a price; therefore glorify [honor] God in [with] your body."

Alfred Heller, an Ohio doctor, takes these verses as the basis for his study of Christian diet and physical fitness, *Your Body, His Temple.*

In the chapter, "Borrowed Property," Heller reminds us of our responsibility as Christians to keep the bodies

God has given us in the best possible condition. Exercise, indeed, is not only a matter of good sense, but it is also, for the believer, an obligation of good management.[19]

There is a somewhat misunderstood reference to exercise in 1 Timothy 4:8: "bodily discipline [exercise] is only of little profit" — a translation which seems to question the value of exercise. Martin Luther's German translation of *wenig nutz* (of little value) carries a similar connotation, and with my Lutheran background I can easily visualize a rather hefty translator-monk minimizing physical activity!

I find the *New International Version* translation, "Physical training is of some value, but godliness has value for all things, holding promise for both the present life and the life to come," truer to the intent of the passage. Paul had great regard for physical activity, as evidenced by his various references to athletics, e.g., 1 Corinthians 9:24.

Suggestions for Enriching Your Study

Develop a practical understanding of the place of exercise in older adult health. Give serious consideration to establishing (or reinforcing) some basic exercise activity.

(a) In regard to health, do you consider yourself a "victim of good living"? Support your answer.

(b) Would you judge the physical benefits of exercise more important to your health than the psychological? Why?

(c) Do a Bible study on a Christian case for exercise.

Chapter Five

TO VITAMIN OR NOT TO VITAMIN

"Food," my mother said firmly, "was meant to be eaten, not to be analyzed." So we ate our breakfast oatmeal without question.

But times have changed, and we have watched a virtual revolution in the understanding and handling of what at one time was a simple matter of "eating our daily bread."

Today such nutrition bywords as "Adelle Davis," "*Prevention* magazine" and "riboflavin" are a normal part of many household discussions. Moreover, minerals such as zinc, iron and magnesium have moved to the classification of food supplement in addition to the category of the metallurgical. Indeed, no longer can you assume that your grandchildren are learning the alphabet when they lisp their *ABCs*. Actually, they could be identifying vitamins.

What does all this mean to us as older adults? Dr. Robert M. Butler, director of the National Institute on Aging, gave a significant answer at the 1977 hearing of the Senate Select Committee on Nutrition and Human Needs:

Proper nutrition throughout life, including in late life, is an effective means of maintaining good health and minimizing degenerative changes in the later years. . . It is only through adequately nutritious diets that older people retain the capacity to remain active and productive.[1]

Commenting further on Butler's statement, Jane Brody writes:

[Good nutrition] may be able to delay or avoid entirely some disorders commonly caused by nutritional deficiencies, including fragile bones and fractures, some forms of senility, chronic constipation, and what could best be called a lack of zest for living. What's more, an improved diet may diminish the older person's risk of developing diabetes, high blood pressure, heart disease, cancer, and stroke.[2]

How challenging to realize the extent to which we can affect our health by how and what we eat! Fortunately, it is never too late to begin an improved nutritional program. The story of Elisabeth will illustrate.

An outstanding cook all of her life, Elisabeth in her seventies was still cooking for a friend with whom she shared a home. But the day came when Elisabeth lost the motivation to continue preparing meals for others and moved into her own apartment. There, with limited companionship and incentive, her own meals became haphazard and nutritionally somewhat bizarre. As a result, she began to deteriorate both physically and mentally. Finally, after several months, she moved again and became a resident in a fine Christian nursing home. The change in her was dramatic. In a relatively short time, with loving care and regular nutritionally sound meals, Elisabeth's physical and mental condition stabilized and her remaining years were satisfying for both her and her family.

As Dr. Butler points out, older adults who are confused, delusional or have serious memory lapses may be suffering from malnutrition and anemia, and the condition often clears up with proper care and nutritious food.

As we consider older adult nutrition these days, however, we face a dilemma. On the one hand, we have a wealth of practical, scientific information on what food is and what constitutes healthy eating. All about us are dietary recommendations, nutrition workshops and the latest word on what is good for us and what is harmful. Yet on the other hand, we are bombarded with a steadily increasing and persistently promoted supply of unhealthy foodstuffs. Brody estimates that "the food industry spends more than $2 billion a year for advertising, mostly pushing the nutritionally deficient ones — snacks, candy, and soft drinks laden with fat, sugar and calories."[3] Even a casual observer of the advertising scene can recognize the massive media food promotion that emphasizes eye and sweet-tooth appeal. Someone has said that the current culinary guide words have become fast, colorful and convenient.

In the introductory chapter to her book on nutrition, Brody notes that Americans are basically ignorant of good nutrition, ". . . at the mercy of . . . food fadists, diet mongers, vitamin hawkers, and self-styled nutritionists."[4]

It seems clear, then, that if we are to remain active and productive as older adults, we must give careful consideration to proper nutrition. So each of us — whatever our capacity and whether as wife, husband, or single — needs to have at least a basic understanding of what constitutes good nutrition. This does not mean to be an expert, but at least to be knowledgeable.

The following five areas give a simple foundation for sound nutritional thinking.

A. Dietary Guidelines[5]

1. Eat a variety of food.
2. Maintain ideal weight.
3. Avoid excessive fat, saturated fat and cholesterol.
4. Eat foods with adequate starch and fiber.
5. Avoid excessive sugar.
6. Avoid excessive sodium (salt).
7. If you drink alcohol, do it in moderation.[6]

B. The Basic Food Groups Chart. The U. S. Department of Agriculture has listed foods in four major areas as a basis for nutritious meal planning. Use of this chart[7] guides toward essential balance and variety in diet.

Group	Foods	Servings	Each Serving Equals:
Milk	whole, skim & low fat milk and its by-products: buttermilk, cheese, cottage cheese, yogurt & ice cream	two or more daily	1 cup milk, 1 cup yogurt, 2 cups cottage cheese 1½ ozs. cheddar cheese, or 1¾ cups ice cream
Meat	poultry, lean meat, fish, eggs, peanut butter, nuts, soy extenders, dried beans & peas, or lentils	two or more daily	2-3 oz. cooked poultry, meat or fish, 2 eggs 4 Tbls. peanut butter, ⅓ cup nuts, or 1 cup cooked dried beans, peas or lentils

Bread/cereal	bread, cereal, graham crackers, saltines, muf-fins, macaroni, noodles, rice, or spaghetti	four or more daily	1 slice bread, ¾ cup dry cereal ½ cup cooked cereal, 2 graham crackers, 1 muffin, or ½ cup macaroni, noodles, rice or spaghetti
Fruit/vegetables: rich in vitamin C	citrus fruit, melon, straw-berries, tomatoes, potatoes	four or more one per day	½ cup fruit, vegetable or juice
rich in vitamin A	broccoli, spin-ach, cress, chard, winter squash, sweet potatoes, pumpkin, apricots, carrots, cantaloupe	at least three per week	½ cup fruit or cooked vegetable
Special need:	Water	4-6 glasses water or juice each day	

C. VITAMIN AND MINERAL VALUE CHART. This chart provides a basic indication of the practical use of the vitamins and minerals listed, as well as their major sources. Helpful suggestions on dosages and combina-tions are found in Mann's chapter on Nutrition and Aging in his *Secrets of Life Extension*.[8]

Vitamin	Importance	Foods found in
Fat (oil)-soluble vitamins —	stored by the body and best assimilated when taken to-gether at meals	

A	eye health (essential for vision in dim light); healthy condition of skin, mucous membranes; formation and maintenance of bone growth	liver, apricots, mangoes, carrots, sweet potatoes, broccoli, spinach, fish oils, milk, butter, egg yolks, tomatoes, cantaloupes
D	anti-stress agent (maintains good amounts of calcium in the blood, which has a calming effect); essential for normal bone growth and maintenance (helps prevent osteoporosis)	fish, liver, eggs, butter
E	helps form red blood cells, muscle and other tissue; aids in protection from ozone damage (decreases oxygen requirement of cells & improves cardiovascular system); helps prevent some types of anemia, cancer and premature aging	whole grain cereals, wheat germ, green leafy vegetables
K	influences body's production of blood clotting proteins	green & yellow vegetables, especially cabbage and spinach

Water-soluble vitamins — excesses are excreted in the urine and perspiration, so should be derived regularly from the diet

B-complex	combats effects of stress when taken in combination; metabolizing energy from carbohydrates, fats & proteins; helps maintain proper functioning of nervous system	

Thiamin (B_1)	helps obtain energy from food	liver, dry peas and beans, whole grain and enriched breads and cereals
Riboflavin (B_2)	helps cells produce energy; essential to many chemical changes in body tissues, as in the absorption of carbohydrates, proteins and fats; aids in correcting or preventing "whistle marks" — wrinkles about the mouth associated with aging women	milk, meat, eggs, dark leafy greens
Niacin (B_3)	needed by cells for the utilization of oxygen to produce energy; protects against stress; reduces fatty deposits in skin & cholesterol accumulations in the arteries; counteracts blood clotting (frequent cause of premature death, stroke, heart attack & loss of normal brain functioning); regresses atherosclerosis & improves circulation	whole grains, fish, poultry, eggs, peanuts
Pantothenic acid (B_5)	outstanding in combating the effects of stress; relieves arthritis; increases stamina; aids in improving memory; acts as laxative in large doses (bran)	liver, brewer's yeast, egg yolks, wheat bran, peas, lima beans, fish

Pydidozine $(B_6$	important anti-stress agent; helps prevent cholesterol accumulation; combined with zinc can help relieve edema during menopause; aids in formation of red blood cells	meats, liver, egg yolks brewer's yeast, whole grains, bananas, vegetables
Cobalamine (B_{12})	essential for normal development of red blood cells and the functioning of the nervous system; aids in insomnia; effective in combating stress and fatigue (large amounts can alleviate exhaustion, increase energy, correct fatigue-induced impotence, and relieve mental symptoms of deficiency)	liver, meats, milk, cheese, eggs
C	*Special:* can protect against, or overcome: diseases & disorders as arthritis, atherosclerosis, many forms of heart disease and the common cold *Every day:* helps maintain normal vision, healthy gums & skin; essential for healing wounds & resistance to infection; increases efficiency of other nutrients; prevents intestional bacteria	citrus fruits, melon, berries, leafy vegetables, tomatoes
Folic Acid	assists in forming body proteins and in the formation of hemoglobin	liver, fruit, yeast, leafy vegetables

Mineral	Importance	Foods found in
Calcium	important for structure and growth of bones and teeth; assists in blood clotting; important for proper functioning of nerves, muscles and heart	milk, cheese, dark leafy greens, sardines, clams, oysters
Copper	aids in the formation of red blood cells and is necessary for the absorption and utilization of iron	oysters, nuts, organ meats, dried peas and beans
Iodine	necessary for the proper functioning of the thyroid gland; contributes to proper metabolism	iodized salt, seafood
Iron	combines with protein in formation of hemoglobin, which carries oxygen from lungs to organs and muscles; prevents anemia; helps release energy from food	liver, lean meats, whole grains, dark green vegetables, eggs, shrimp, oysters
Magnesium	plays a role in the metabolism of calcium and potassium; contributes to normal functioning of nervous and muscular systems; aids in maintaining acid-alkaline balance; essential for the utilization of protein	whole grains, nuts, sesame seeds, dark green vegetables, seafood, soy flour
Phosphorus	works with calcium in maintenance of bones and teeth; helps to store and release energy	milk, cheese, meat, fish, poultry, grains, nuts (almost all foods)

| Selenium | helps in prevention of heart disease, cancer, arthritis, rheumatism attacks, atherosclerosis and poor circulation; retards aging process | fish, poultry, meats, grains, milk, vegetables |
| Zinc | promotes rapid healing of broken bones, burns, cuts and bruises; benefits immune system; helps break down fats and lowers cholesterol; assists in preventing age-induced prostatitis and rheumatoid arthritis; required for proper taste perception | milk, liver, shell-fish, herring, wheat brans, beans, eggs |

D. SAMPLE ADULT NUTRITIONAL MENU.   This gives ideas for balanced food planning.[9]

General suggestions:

- Get your essential proteins from stews, hearty broths, flaked fish, or purees of meat, eggs, milk, cereal, and gelatins.
- Relieve intestinal problems with the natural roughage of fruits, vegetables.
- Avoid fried foods or rich sauces.
- Since warm foods or beverages are more easily digested than cold, start meals with soup or a warm beverage.
- Eat at least three meals a day.

Suggested Menu

6 A.M. Warm beverage — tea, coffee or hot milk
8 A.M. Citrus fruit or juice
        Iron-fortified cereal or soft-boiled egg

Toast and butter or margarine
Tea, coffee, cocoa, or skim milk

Noon   Cream or thick vegetable soup or juice
Sandwich of meat, fish, egg, cheese, or
peanut butter on whole-wheat bread
Green vegetable or raw salad
Stewed fruit, rice pudding, or tapioca

3 P.M.   Broth, milk, or hot chocolate
Toast or crackers

6 P.M.   Minced chicken, lamb, or broiled ham-
burger
Potato, baked or mashed, or rice
Cooked vegetable, green or yellow
Toast with butter or margarine
Custard, plain cake, or fruit
Beverage

Nourishing food and proper eating habits can reverse
the downward spiral of depression and apathy which is
aggravated by decreasing interest in food.

E. NUTRITIONAL CONCERNS

1. *Calories.* Weight control is a continuing American problem, and the market is filled with reducing
plans and programs. In fact, a wag has suggested
that the simplest reduction program would be the
exercise involved in carting about a week's supply
of new programs!

We all have some concern with the cosmetic
value of a shapely bod. Indeed, as one health authority has noted, that most effective reducing motivation
is still "the view in the bathroom mirror." However,
even for those for whom the swimming pool appearance is no longer a consuming incentive, there is a
far more relevant calorie concern. It is found in the
reminder that being overweight "aggravates diabetes,

high blood pressure, and heart disease, and contributes to digestive and kidney disease; it increases one's vulnerability during surgery . . . and seriously overweight people are more susceptible to certain cancers and fatal accidents."[10]

As you can see, controlling weight has considerably more than cosmetic value! And, while being overweight produces difficulties at any age, increasing age and the resultant body changes greatly aggravate those difficulties.

For many, the answer is some form of diet. As one authority suggests, "There is a 'diet' in circulation to suit every taste, every budget, and every misconception. There are fat farms and diet pills, 'miracle' waist trimmers and sugarless fudge. There are 'natural' approaches and unabashedly unnatural ones. There are mental attitudes . . . reducing groups that combine the rituals of the confessional and the pep rally. Acupuncture is touted by some, hypnosis by others. And for the desperate, there are truly desperate measures: sleep cures, jaw wiring, even gastric stapling."[11]

Gastric stapling?

Although the focus of this chapter is sound nutrition rather than weight control, there are some basic principles relating to such control:

> (a) Effective weight control must begin with adequate motivation. (This touches on behavior modification principles which emphasize that it is not merely a matter of spasmodically losing pounds, only to gain them back, but establishing a life style that distinguishes between eating to satisfy energy and health needs and eating to satisfy emotional or other needs.[12]

(b) Establish a sound nutritional eating program as a base for weight control (avoid extremes).

(c) Combine suitable exercise with the eating program.

2. *Food preparation.* Healthy cooking methods are broiling, baking, steaming and boiling. The contemporary use of microwave cooking has advantages for both speed and food value, as well as flavor. Durk Pearson and Sandy Shaw maintain that the carcinogen production in microwaved meat is negligible, and that microwaving is the least destructive of vitamins.[13]

3. *To vitamin or not to vitamin.* Do we get sufficient nutrients directly from our foods, or do we need to include vitamin/mineral supplements?

Certainly a well-chosen diet from varied sources is the ideal approach, and vitamin pills cannot make up for a faulty diet. But unfortunately, as Heller points out, "we do not live in an ideal world. American food production and distribution is highly centralized; so-called fresh fruits and vegetables lose some of their nutrients as they travel long distances to market. Even if we eat only home-grown food, modern environmental factors may inhibit our ability to absorb fully essential nutrients or may increase our need for them. The effects of untested chemicals, pesticidal residues, pollution, and stress are factors which affect vitamin-mineral absorption." He further suggests that "used sensibly, nutritional supplements are cheap protection against the ill-understood ravages of modern society."[14]

God has given us bodies which are wonderfully and fearfully made, but He expects us to maintain them properly. As we seek His guidance, He can give us the desire for nutritious food, but it is our responsibility to learn what that is, how to select it for a daily balanced diet, and how to prepare it properly.

God prospered and blessed Daniel's wise choice of food (Daniel 1:8-16), and surely He will add enjoyment to our older adult lives as good nutrition becomes a means of effectively maintaining the body, His temple!

Suggestions for Enriching Your Study

Develop sufficient understanding of nutrition to make eating a consistently enjoyable, healthful experience. Eating is a part of adult life over which, with a bit of effort, we can exercise considerable control.

(a) To evaluate your nutritional health, do a simple three-day review of your meals, using the Basic Four Food Groups Chart (B) to get a general picture of how consistently you are eating balanced meals.

(b) Take time to review the Vitimin and Mineral Chart (C) for any personal difficulties that might be aided by dietary means. (Please note that while this material is based on reliable sources, it is in no way intended as a substitute for official medical information.)

(c) Do a Bible study for a Christian approach to nutrition.

(Research and charts for this chapter were prepared by Marjorie M. Graendorf.)

Chapter Six

BUT WHAT DO YOU DO WITH THE WHEELS?

The decision to live our retirement years in a mobile home was not without its reservations. Where, for example, do you store those big mobile home trailer wheels if you have only a carport?

Or there was the day my former teaching colleague wrote to congratulate us on now "being able to pick up your house and travel." (When that note came, I remember going outside to stare at our sixty-five-foot long mobile and wondering how the family Pontiac would manage to roll it down the highway.) Obviously, many still equate mobile-home living with the recreational vehicle of the 70s — aluminum siding, bottled gas and all.

We have since realized the truth of J. J. Kramer's introductory note in his *Mobile Home Guide:* "Forget anything and everything you have ever heard or read about yesterday's mobile home."[1]

That's not hard to do as I sit here in our 1650 square feet of cathedral-ceilinged mobile, the fire crackling cheerily in our great room fireplace.

And the trailer wheels? Not to worry; the mobile manufacturer keeps them. We expect to stay on our present site. No trailer traveling here; less than two percent of this type of housing is ever moved.

It's time to clarify some terms. The word "mobile" originally identified this as moveable housing, which is the basis for much of the misconception of mobile living as transient. Happily, the term has been updated by the 1980 government Housing Act, which officially defined this type of housing as manufactured homes. So we now speak more accurately of this kind of home as being factory built (manufactured), rather than emphasizing its moveability (mobile). The various terms will, of course, continue to be used somewhat interchangeably for a time.

In contrast to manufactured/mobile, the standard type of housing is usually identified as site built; that is, the house basically is built on the lot. It is the type of building in which most of us probably grew up.

There is a wide range of housing possibilities for the older adult. Besides the single-dwelling home, there are condominiums, apartments, duplexes, retirement hotels and retirement communities, share-a-home programs, and a steadily increasing array of housing possibilities. One of the housing projections of the future is a combination of site-built and manufactured building. It has been pioneered by such builders as Sonoma International (The Fifty/Fifty House) and Lusk-Fleetwood.

A preliminary decision on retirement housing concerns whether or not to move from your present location. A relatively small percentage of retired couples do move to new locations (less than 5 percent). Among the major considerations for those making a move are: preference for a smaller home (less upkeep, less need for space with children out of the house); preference for a single-story place to avoid stairs; negative neighborhood changes; house deterioration and repair needs; desire for a climate change.

For many, proximity to children is a prime consideration. However, keep in mind that this is not always the best basis for a major move. As the AIM retirement planning booklet suggests, "You may find that your children's friends aren't your friends; that their way of living is not your way of living; that you may be more a convenient baby-sitter than an honored guest; and finally, that they may be transferred or decide to relocate soon after you make your move."[2]

If you do move, there are critical concerns. Housing for most of us represents one of the major financial investments of our life.

A basic consideration is *location*. Where will you spend what may be the major portion of your remaining years? Keep in mind that this represents more than just geography. As the AARP retirement housing guide well states, "Remember that housing is not just the roof over your head. It is a life style."[3]

In his well-known study on developmental tasks, educator Robert Havighurst has a helpful section on the tasks (what you need to accomplish for effective personal development at various life stages) for later maturity. He describes one such task for older adulthood as being "to establish satisfactory physical living arrangements." Under this task are these factors to consider:

1. Quietness
2. Privacy
3. Independence
4. Nearness to relatives and friends
5. Residence among own cultural group
6. Cheapness (reasonable cost; consider taxes and maintenance)
7. Proximity to transportation and communal institutions[4]

(Most of these factors relate to housing locality.)

A prime suggestion is to get as much information as possible before making a decision on *location*. Avoid any final determination on the basis of nostolgia (what you remember from back when — things usually have changed); on brief encounters (that happy vacation visit — you may have snow in the winter); and somebody else's enthusiastic recommendation (the salesman's brother-in-law).

Most housing advisors recommend spending enough time in a projected living location to have a feel for seasonal changes, as well as neighborhood setting and activity. (We recently had word of friends who relocated at considerable effort and expense, only to discover that the husband is allergic to the climate conditions of the season they did not observe.)

So check local newspapers, talk with local residents, visit the area in some depth, consider the possibility of renting before buying if there are uncertainties.

A second important consideration relates to the *type* of housing, and this will involve such concerns as cost, proximity to others and ownership responsibilities.

A third area of concern takes in the field of *furnishings and equipment*.

Joseph Michaels, in his *Prime of Your Life,* a guide for mature years, emphasizes the importance of adequate lighting: "You should have . . . good-sized windows in all rooms as well as proper fixtures . . . Windows are for visual communication as well as light, even if it amounts to nothing more than looking out and watching other people go about their daily tasks."[5]

Further vital considerations include such things as grab bars for bathtubs and bathroom areas, non-slip floors and convenient, easy-to-reach storage areas.

Keep in mind that in terms of long-range use the housing may serve, by stages, adults who are considered active, slowing down or even convalescent. It usually pays to anticipate potential use.

In summary, as you consider retirement living arrangements, there are three main guidelines to keep in mind — the three Cs of effective older adult housing: comfort, convenience and cost.

Comfort. The aging process sometimes includes aching toes and hurting elbows. Remember your physical conditions and needs as you choose housing. Talk with others who have similar situations. Keep in mind the housing layout and furniture that will make your second fifty years as comfortable as possible. Often this is not a matter of increased expense as much as it is of foresight.

Some people keep what they call a NETA (*Next Time Around*) file, a collection of reminders on what they would do differently or improve in the future.

Convenience. We remember the couple who happily invested in a lovely multi-story home for their retirement, never considering the husband's lame leg. No big problem at fifty-five. But stairs eventually became an increasing burden. Best advice — stay with one level, avoid extensive landscaping commitments, plan for compact kitchens. Build and buy for the conveniences that, without being labeled luxuries, help make you a more effective person in living a productive life.

Cost. Keep in mind retirement income and economic fluctuations. It is here that manufactured/mobile housing can be a viable factor. As Kramer notes: "Mobile homes offer one of the lowest initial costs and lowest maintenance costs of the various types of housing available."

The Lord's Word on Housing

As in all major decisions relating to living, the Lord has something encouraging for us with regard to housing.

First, as God's people (those who are in Christ, covered by His righteousness), we have His assurance that

He blesses (does good) for our homes. "He blesses the home of the righteous" (Proverbs 3:33b, NIV).

While there is no specific direction on what type of house to buy, there is admonition to have a well-built one, as in Christ's story of the wise housebuilder who was commended for building solidly (Matthew 7:24,25). The parable of the man who built his house upon the rock has the spiritual application of building life on a good foundation. But the principle certainly carries over to any type of building. Establish your home on a good foundation; have housing, as well as living, well built.

There is another biblical housing principle. Here in California we live in earthquake country. That is always a reminder that the human building — houses as well as bodies — are temporary. So the Word reminds us that "If the earthly house [Paul appropriately, calls it a tent] is destroyed, we have a building from God, an eternal house in heaven, not built by human hands" (2 Corinthians 5:1, NIV)

Finally, there are the moving words of Jesus, "Do not let your hearts be troubled. . . . In My Father's house are many dwelling places" [places for living, rooms] (John 14:1).

The shepherd king of the Old Testament, David, expressed it in the 23rd Psalm. "The Lord," he wrote, "is my shepherd [caretaker] . . . I will dwell in the house of the LORD forever" — a permanent place to live, eternal housing!

Suggestions for Enriching Your Study

Establish some practical principles for guidance in choosing and maintaining your living arrangements.

(a) Which of the 3 Cs of guidelines for older adult living arrangements (comfort, convenience, cost) is most helpful for you?

(b) Take time to visit and evaluate at least three of the types of housing possibilities noted. (Choose types you would consider using.)

(c) In anticipation of retirement, make a chart listing reasons you would or would not move from your present location.

Chapter Seven

NO TIME FOR RUSTING!

Noted Christian author, Bruce Larson, closes his book, *There's a Lot More to Health Than Not Being Sick,* with the challenging story of Lena Fletcher.

Lena, an 84-year-old lady in the Seattle area who worked daily in her garden, had a very practical approach to aging: "Other people jog to keep fit. I work in the garden and split and pile wood. It makes a lot more sense to have something to show for the energy you expend!"

"One day," commented Larson, "Lena Fletcher will die. But I don't believe she will ever be old."[1]

I like that. Lena had no time for rusting!

There are two ways of handling our later years. I call them the TIC and TAC approaches — taken from the game of tic-tac-toe. TIC represents *The Inactive Calendar* approach of zeroes, and TAC is for *The Active Calendar* of crosses.

In good gerontological (the study of aging) language, we are talking about the two major theories on how to age: *disengagement* (TIC) and *activity* (TAC).

K. Warner Schaie identifies disengagement as "a feeling that aging is . . . a time to slow down. Activities should be curtailed, and friends should be reduced in number to a more manageable collection."[2]

In contrast, activity theory is explained as keeping active, ". . . continually finding new interests to replace work, and new friends to replace those who have moved or passed away."[3]

What kind of lives do we anticipate as older adults?

When my father-in-law took early retirement after a full, busy life, he and I managed an occasional round of golf together. It was his basic retirement activity, and he was good at it. However, since Dad had very little else to occupy his days, time often hung heavy on his hands.

Here indeed is one of the major challenges faced by the older adult — how to keep alive the spark of meaningful activity.

"Without things to do, a person goes to seed and his health suffers. Everyone needs something to do, whether it is reading, study, church work, volunteering, a hobby, a sport, taking part in a community activity or, best of all, enjoying a variety of active interests and affairs."[4]

For most of us, life in our childhood and youth had little room for monotony. There were school activities and vacations, followed by the years of courtship and family. As young adults, we were caught up with our vocation and the daily challenge of making a living.

But suddenly we are older adults, and the adventure fades a bit. Life slows down and becomes routine and, possibly, monotonous.

I remember a seminary professor of mine who always had a spark about him. Life seemed to contain endless opportunity for former college president J. Oliver Buswell, and there was always more to be done than time in which to do it.

One day in class he told us that he planned to ask the Lord for permission to use the first one thousand years of his time in eternity to catch up on reading all the good books he hadn't had time to enjoy during his days on earth!

Robert Louis Stevenson wrote, "The world is so full of a number of things, I'm sure we should all be as happy as kings."

The creator has indeed provided us with a remarkable world — actually a number of worlds.

There is, for instance, the enchanting world of reading. One of the delights for the older adult is the opportunity for leisurely book perusal. I am finding this to be true.

Some years ago a family friend in Pasadena turned over to me her set of the Harvard Classics, that intriguing "five-foot shelf" of the world's great literature. After thanking my gracious friend profusely, I allowed the gift to suffer, what is, unfortunately, the fate of many book sets — boxing and storage until "some day."

Well, among the book boxes that appeared when we moved to our present manufactured home was — you guessed it — the Harvard Classics. Great. But where do you put a five-foot shelf of books in a house already occupied by the home and office library of a retired teacher?

But the Lord had anticipated our needs. The previous owner of our mobile home had opted for a built-in desk with two built-in book shelves instead of the usual built-in bar. Perfect.

Now I'm enjoying the Harvard Classics. The first volume, for instance, contains Benjamin Franklin's *Autobiography*. Remember some of his sayings from Poor

Richard's Almanack: "He that riseth late, must trot all day . . ." "God helps them that help themselves;" "Plough deep while Sluggards sleep . . ." "Little Strokes Fell great Oaks."

Incidentally, a helpful (not easy) volume on reading books is Mortimer Adler's *How to Read a Book,* where he points out that effective reading is the heart of an education and subtitles his volume on reading as "The Art of Getting a Liberal Education."[5] We can continue to learn.

Speaking of education, another enjoyable older adult activity is traveling — not just to add another baggage sticker to the suitcase, but visiting new places to become acquainted with other parts of our world.

We were fortunate on our first trip to Europe to become acquainted with a couple in which the wife was a grade school teacher. As part of her fifth grade teaching experience, she had developed a delightful storehouse of information about every facet of our trip. I'll tell you, we got to know the inside story of each *schloss* on the Rhine from Cologne to Kobelintz!

Suggestion: Take time to anticipate your travel. Some research can enrich every part of the trip.

Of course, travel involves the pocketbook. Or does it? We spent a delightful low-budget vacation one summer becoming acquainted with the world within fifty miles of our home. It is surprising how many people we have introduced to some of the sights in their own area! I remember, for instance, taking my seminary roommate, who lived in New York City, to the Empire State Building!

Worlds of activity. All around us are opportunities such as reading and traveling for the useful investment of our time. For many folks there is the thoroughly enjoyable possibility of gardening, which can be both scenic in terms of flowers and edible in terms of fresh fruits and vegetables. The field of collecting ranges from the familiar coin collecting (numistics) and stamp gathering (philately) to collecting and polishing rocks (lapidary).

There is painting, sculpting, needlecraft, woodworking and carving, and a virtually unlimited array of arts, crafts and hobbies. The outdoorsman enjoys fishing and such related activities as fly-tying.

A growing field for adult activity is adult education, with a huge selection of subjects and programs being offered by almost every sizeable community.

As the older adult population grows, there are increasing opportunities for church and community service. There are such areas, for example, as the volunteer secretarial work that can be a boon to the struggling pastor of a small church.

One retired couple enjoys keeping their church grounds in showplace condition.

I remember the housebound saint who used her telephone for a daily ministry of cheer and visitation.

My study contains a bookcase that represents a ministry of love by a dear older carpenter in the church.

My dentist returned recently from several weeks of donated dentistry on a South American mission field.

Worlds of activity. All around us are opportunities for the investment of our time. Meaningful investment. Note that we are not talking here about simply finding something to do. We can spend our time doing something of value, and that does not mean just making money. There are other values than the financial.

There can be the legitimate value of relaxation. In the early thirties, Edmund Jacobson wrote his classic study on the art of relaxing, *You Must Relax.* The subtitle for the book was "Reducing the Strains of Modern Living."[6] That was fifty years ago; the space age has not reduced those strains! I once read a news item about a man in New York who was hospitalized for a nervous breakdown when he missed one section of a revolving door.

The tensions of daily living are not new to our age. Jesus spoke to His disciples about the need for relaxing "because so many people were coming and going that they did not even have a chance to eat, He said to them, 'Come with me by yourselves to a quiet place, and get some rest'" (Mark 6:31, NIV). A writer has suggested that the King James translation of "Come ye yourselves apart" leads naturally to the conclusion, "or you will come apart"! Anyhow, you'll remember, the group took a boat trip to an out-of-the-way area, where the feeding of the five thousand took place.

"Take time," says the poet, "to smell the roses." We do get involved with the mundane, don't we? I complimented my neighbor recently on an exquisite white rose in his front yard. "What white rose?" he replied, as he hastened off to his job at the office.

Here are some activity guidelines, some suggestions for discovering and developing areas of interest.

(a) *Investigate.* There are potential activity opportunities all around us. Begin with present contacts such as churches, neighborhood clubs and the news media. Visit the often neglected but potentially most useful information resource — the local library. Use your phone, too.

(b) *Evaluate.* Review your own interests. What contacts have you had in the past? What did you enjoy doing at one time? Get some fresh ideas. Evaluate in terms of your abilities, companionship, equipment needs and cost.

(c) *Initiate.* Get acquainted with possibilities. Observe what others are doing. Do some visiting (most groups welcome guests). Get some training. Do some reading. (Remember the library?) Expose yourself to suggestions from friends and fellow workers. Try something. You may surprise yourself!

Suggestions for Enriching Your Study

We have a major challenge as older adults to remain usefully active persons. It is a worthwhile effort.

(a) On the basis of a minimal schedule of personal responsibilities, lay out a program of what you would consider worthwhile retirement activity.

(b) From a Christian older adult perspective, do you consider it more challenging to handle an extremely full activity schedule or an extremely slack one? Why?

(c) Take time to learn one new hobby or craft (or further develop one you already know).

UNIT THREE

Productive Aging

UNIT THREE
Productive Aging . . .

Jesus grew in wisdom (Luke 2:52, NIV).
Keep on the alert (Mark 13:33).

Whatever else you forgot in Alexander Grigolia's college anthropology class, you could never forget *him*. Attending one of his classes was an exciting experience!

There was, for example, the day in class that he introduced us to his staff "assistant," Josephine, while fondly holding her hand. Now understand, it wasn't so much the matter of a professor holding an assistant's hand that disturbed the students that morning. After all, we were a liberated group of collegians (we thought).

But the fact that Josephine was a five-foot laboratory skeleton was something else. Her abrupt appearance that day out of the classroom closet, kept several students thoroughly awake the rest of the semester!

As memorable as anything else connected with the class, however, was the celebrated professor's unique introduction to his course tests. Putting on his most soulful look, he would regularly precede any test announcement with the reminder, in his doleful Russian accent, that "Life, peoples, is a stroogle for existence."

The expression itself came from Charles Darwin's famous study on evolution in *The Origin of Species,* where he tried to explain why living things developed. For those who took Dr. Grigolia's tests, Darwin's works had a more personal significance as we had our private struggle with Anthropology 326 from week to week.

For many older adults, life is likewise a struggle — a struggle for meaning. It is easy to lose the zest for life that at one time made it worthwhile. Days can tend to drag, and nights sometimes hang heavily.

Happy, therefore, is the older person who continues to find living an adventure! It is here we often begin to realize that effective aging is not only a matter of keeping the body in shape, but it also is the challenge of keeping the mind alert, living a useful life.

Beyond confident and healthy living, successful aging includes *Productive* aging.

Note the challenge of the biblical writer Paul in the book of Ephesians, as he encourages us to "live life, then, with a due sense of responsibility, not as men who do not know the meaning and purpose of life, but as those who do. Make the best use of your time, despite all the difficulties" (Ephesians 5:15,16, Phillips *New Testament in Modern English*).

Here is Paul's great 3M formula for a productive life!

It begins with "knowing the *meaning* and *purpose* of life," as explained in chapter 8. Get up each day with a reason for living!

It continues in chapter 9 with the *M* of *motivation* — "live with a sense of responsibility."

Finally, in chapter 10 there is the *M* of *management of time* — make the best use of your time despite difficulties."

Chapter Eight

A REASON FOR LIVING

The story is told that during the early stages of building the great cathedral of Cologne in Germany, the workers became discontented. That was not surprising. Hauling the bricks was back-breaking drudgery. The weather along the Rhine River, where Cologne is located, could not be trusted. Dust from digging foundation trenches made breathing difficult. All of that, along with minimal wages, contributed to a thoroughly miserable situation.

Yet in the midst of it all, the story has it that among the workmen one man reacted differently from the others. Gregor actually seemed to enjoy his work! Occasionally he whistled, and often a smile creased his broad German face. The contrast in attitude became increasingly noticeable to the other men, and one day as the men ate their lunches, Rudolf, an older laborer, could contain his curiosity no longer.

"Tell me, Gregor," he queried. "Why is it that as we work at this miserable job day after day, you are able to remain cheerful among the bricks and dirt?"

Gregor hesitated a moment. Then he spoke quietly.

"I will tell you, Rudolf," he said. "I met the *baumeister* (architect) one morning several months ago when he was inspecting the work, and I complained about what we had to do.

"He listened to me. Then he explained what we actually were doing.

"'Our purpose here,' he said, 'is not just to haul bricks. We are together building a cathedral to the glory of God.'

"And that, of course," continued Gregor, "is what makes the work worthwhile. It is one thing to be a workman in a Cologne brickyard. It is quite something else to be building a cathedral for God's glory!"

Here, similarly, is our challenge as Christians. You and I are more than just passing hod carriers in a vague enterprise. Paul the apostle identifies us as "God's fellow-workers" (1 Corinthians 3:9) who are together engaged in building His kingdom. We have a high calling.

When I graduated from college, one of my professors, J. L. Leedy, wrote in my yearbook a bit of Browning, which I've never forgotten. It was the quotation that a man's reach should exceed his grasp. Paul had expressed it this way: "I press on toward the goal" (Philippians 3:14).

The longer we live the more we become aware of the challenge to make our lives count. I remember so well the somewhat time-tattered placard on the kitchen wall of my parents' midwestern home: *Only One Life, 'Twill Soon Be Past, Only What's Done for Christ Will Last.*

The early Presbyterians put it a bit more theologically in their catechism where the familiar question about the chief end (purpose) of man is answered simply, ". . . to glorify God, and to enjoy him for ever."

Paul himself had established that when he wrote to the believers in the Greek city of Corinth, ". . . whatever you do, do all to the glory of God" (1 Corinthians 10:31).

Pictured here is a person who seeks to live his daily life in such a way that God is honored by it as his purpose is fulfilled through it.

Three basic steps are involved. The first is an overall Christian *commitment,* a conscious giving of one's *life* to God, through Jesus Christ.

The second is *dedicating* each new *day* and its activities to Him.

The third is *implementing* my desire to fulfill His purposes by regularly seeking *direction* through God's Word, God's presence and God's people. Included, too, is setting and accomplishing goals in my life.

Setting a goal needs to be *specific* (write it down) and *practical* (give it a time-orientation).

There are a great number of helpful books on goal setting. I have found Dayton and Engstrom's *Strategy for Living* useful. There are some good thoughts, for example, on the value of goal setting: "Goals give us the ability to take the emphasis off the negative — problems of the present — and focus our thinking on the positive — future possibilities . . . motivation to move forward."[1]

Goals help point us toward a purposeful life. Two illustrations come to mind. The first is the legendary singing cowboy, Gene Autry, whose Anaheim baseball club (the California Angels) is located a few miles from our Brea home. In a recent interview, seventy-five-year-old Autry expressed his personal approach to aging. It was simply to "keep active and keep setting goals."

The second illustration is J. Oswald Sanders, the octogenarian mission executive-author. Like Autry, he combines goals and action.

Sanders was for many years director of Overseas Missionary Fellowship. He "retired" from this to become, at age seventy, principal of a training college in New Guinea. Once again retiring, he became the consulting director of OMF while continuing an extensive speaking-writing career at eighty years of age.

A purposeful life — what a great challenge, regardless of age! As in the case of the Cologne workman, our purpose as believers is more than simply being space occupiers. We are building (living) for God's glory, and that is a majestic reason for living.

While *purpose* represents a more general statement of direction, *goals* are specific steps toward carrying out the purpose.

This matter of clarifying your purpose in life and taking time to spell out specific goals to work toward is exceedingly practical, as the Bible often demonstrates.

The story of Daniel is a good example. Here was a Jewish lad who had been captured by the Babylonians under Nebuchadnezzar. As part of Daniel's retraining program, he was given a special menu. The food was good, but as biblical experts suggest, it was probably food not in keeping with Jewish dietary regulations.

Accordingly, Daniel established his purpose to honor God by not eating the Babylonian diet. As the Bible account states it, "Daniel made up his mind' (Daniel 1:8) not to give up his convictions. One of his goals toward accomplishing his purpose was to demonstrate his ability to survive. It was a well worked-out goal. Notice how it is stated in Daniel 1:12,13: "Please test your servants for ten days . . . then let our appearance be observed . . . and deal with your servants accordingly."

There is no question about what Daniel wanted to accomplish, or the procedure, and he indeed met his goal and dramatically fulfilled his purpose.

As the record finally shows, the king to whom he was accountable found him an exceptional person "in every matter of wisdom and understanding about which the king questioned them [Daniel and the other Jewish men] . . . ten times better than all the magicians and enchanters in his whole kingdom" (Daniel 1:20, NIV). What a testimony!

Daniel was a young man then. But as already noted, the challenge of purposeful living is not restricted to any particular age. It is never too late to initiate, or reemphasize, the determination to make the remainder of your life count. God uses our life *as* we give it to Him, *when* we give it to Him.

We can become cathedral builders at any stage in life!

Suggestions for Enriching Your Study

As a serious Christian it is profitable to establish (or update) purpose in living.

(a) Try to come up with a personal example that illustrates the practical difference between just carrying bricks and building a cathedral.

(b) Informally discuss with a friend the idea of having a purpose for older adult living.

(c) Do some Bible study to identify goals in the lives of several Bible characters, such as Paul.

Chapter Nine

HOW'S YOUR MOTOR-VATION?

"What helps you get things done?" his teacher asked little Johnnie.

Johnnie's answer was better than he realized.

"We need," he stated, "motorvation."

He meant, of course, *moti*vation. But I still like his answer.

A motor is something that gets things moving. We may have goals. But it's another thing to get the motor going to move us toward accomplishing those goals.

Don't we all have lists of projects which never get done — letters to write, gardens to weed, exercise to initiate? What happens? Someone has expressed it this way: It may be great to have the car packed and the vacation route laid out, but you'll never go on that trip until you put gas in the tank and start the motor.

Aha. Getting the motor started. How do we do that?

The psychologist Abraham Maslow made a study of why we do what we do, and the motivation theory that resulted has become a classic in the field.[1]

We have, says Maslow, basic needs which become our stimuli (drives) for action. As example, the need for food (hunger) motivates us to obtain and eat meals. This represents the filling of a basic *physiological* need that we all have.

There are likewise *psychological* needs, such as the need to belong.

This points up the two major types of motivation: (a) external or physical (where the "push" come from outside), and (b) internal or mental (where the "push" comes from inside).

Both types of motivation involve action. In the case of hunger, for example, we are motivated to earn money for buying food. In the same way, the need for belonging might provide encouragement to join a church or club.

The external is the more visible type of motivation, and our early life is guided by this type. Naturally, parents are central in early motivation ("eat your spinach," "time for bed," "brush you teeth," "do your homework.") So we grow up with parent-initiated drives for becoming healthy, useful individuals.

But there comes a time when parental-based motivation is no longer present as we leave home for college or marriage. This means that we must now substitute our own drives, and these become more internal in nature. So if we now eat spinach, we no longer do it because of parental urging, but because of an appreciation for its value. We have *internalized* our motivation. We act because of an inner voice, rather than a spoken one.

But what about the older adult and motivation? First, as we become older, we lose some of the urgency of youth. We no longer "have to" do certain things. Such activity as eating for proper nutrition loses much of its urgency. Exercise can be put off. The sense of freedom on retirement can remove much external motivation.

The Swiss doctor-psychologist, Paul Tournier, in his book *Learn to Grow Old*, points out that retired people can be "like a car that has broken down. Without the motive power [remember Johnnie's motorvation?] in their lives that has been hitherto provided by work they are depressed, resigned, or in revolt."[2]

On the other hand, there are the people who enjoy their retirement thoroughly. As Tournier points out, these are the ones who spontaneously find useful and interesting things to do and are never bored. They have "go" power, enthusiasm about life and living.

Motivation is basically encouragement. It means having a positive answer to the question of getting things done, and your own enthusiasm is a basic key.

First of all, this can represent *direct* action. My father was very good at this. Although he wore suspenders rather than a belt all his life, Dad was always able to provide motivation for his son when needed!

All of us are aware of *direct* motivation. For example, if we feel the need for a more extensive exercise program we might use the motivation of a television program to provide the necessary encouragement.

It could be "The Frisky Limber Up Hour," available at a convenient time, geared to our capabilities, with a lively, enthusiastic exercise leader and the further incentive of appropriate music. And despite our reluctance, we find ourselves doing the difficult body movements we realize are good for us! Direct motivation.

But many of us also have learned to use *secondary* motivation. This is where we get our motivation indirectly. Let me illustrate.

Exercising for some individuals can be very much a matter of mood. We go great for several days, but then come the slow days when the "go" power just isn't there. Yet health experts remind us of the importance of a regular exercise schedule.

Thinking about this one day, I suddenly realized that in having my morning newspaper delivered, I actually was paying the newsboy, not only for delivering the paper, but also for getting *his* daily exercise.

The answer, of course, was to get part of *my* exercise by walking to the newsstand to buy the morning paper. The motivation was to get the daily paper, but in the process I also got regular exercise. Secondary motivation. Think about it. For several years now I have rarely missed either newspaper or walking.

It is surprising how much we can accomplish with sufficient motivation. The classic illustration is the story of the rancher who got trapped one day in his pasture by an angry bull. The only safe spot between the bull and a distant escape fence was a good-sized ground hole. A nearby farmer happened to go by the scene and watched in fascination as the trapped rancher popped out of his hole and tried several times to reach the safety of the fence. Each time, however, the bull managed to cut off the rancher, who jumped back into his hole. With amazing persistence, the rancher continued to pop up to make another run for the fence.

Figuring the rancher was trying to prove he could outlast the bull, the farmer finally decided to lend some encouragement. "Great example of power of motivation, John," he yelled to his neighbor.

To which the rancher quickly yelled back, "Motivation, nothing. There's a bobcat in that hole!"

My brother-in-law has supplied a personally outstanding example of the power of motivation. Some years ago Frank and I were in the California High Sierra country, fishing the Owens River out of Bishop. It was not a good fishing day, and although we knew there were brown trout in the stream, we hadn't been able to prove it!

We were about to call it quits when I became aware of some movement in the meadow grass alongside the stream. A few casual kicks quickly showed the presence of some lively grasshoppers. As every knowledgeable fisherman knows, there's little better trout bait than hoppers. So in a few minutes a revitalized couple of fishermen were having the time of their lives!

However, in the excitement Frank and I got separated. And for Frank that had the potential for tragedy.

Frank, you see, had lost his right arm in the war. So when we separated that afternoon it meant he now had to chase, snag, box, isolate and hook those wiggling hoppers by himself with his one good hand.

Now, I have watched two-handed fishermen exercise almost total effort to handle grasshopper fishing effectively. But a one-handed grasshopper fisherman — seemingly impossible. . .

Except there were those fighting brown trout. I've never been completely sure how he did it, but we had freshly caught trout for supper that evening — caught, if you will, by a one-armed, grasshopper-fishing sportsman.

The power of motivation; it is something to see!

For the Christian believer there is a spiritual dimension to motivation, as exemplified in the experience of Paul the Apostle. Paul faced constant physical as well as spiritual challenge. (Note his personal autobiography of sufferings, for instance, in 2 Corinthians 11 and 12.) In it all, the apostle was motivated to endure through his spiritual resources. "I can do all things," he wrote, "through Christ" (Philippians 4:13, KJV).

A beautiful contemporary illustration is the story of quadriplegic Joni Eareckson Tada.[3]

There is also the spiritual reinforcement of determination. I remember hearing the Chinese evangelist Leland Wang some years ago in college chapel tell about his determination to study the Word of God faithfully. But having an exceedingly full schedule, Wang had found that unless he did his Bible reading early in the morning, it didn't get done. So he established a motivational basis — no Bible, no breakfast — which for some months became a familiar campus byword.

Then, there is the motivational influence of *love.* Thus, the Wycliffe Bible Commentary, for example, interprets the passage in 2 Corinthians 5:14, "the love of Christ controls us" as "motivated by love."

This is ultimate motivation, the controlling, compelling force of love — a mother's love for her child, the Savior's love for His redeemed, the Christian's love for others. The supreme expression, of course, it stated in John 3:16, "for God so loved, . . . that He gave . . . "

Some are blessed with a good deal of natural will power and get a lot done just by deciding to do it. But many of us need that extra push. We still have things to accomplish. As my teenage friend would say, "Go for it!"

Suggestions for Enriching Your Study

A challenge for older adults is to understand and learn to apply some practical motivational principles — how to get going.

(a) Try to recall an example of internalized motivation from your own experience.

(b) What kind of motivation do you see in the older adult Caleb's willingness to tackle the rugged hill country for his inheritance? (Joshua 14.)

(c) Prayerfully apply the motivational strength expressed in Philippians 4:13 to a personal difficulty.

Chapter Ten

THE GIFT OF TIME

9:00 to 9:15 A.M.

I've dusted my desk and I've wound up my watch,
I've tightened (then loosened) my belt by a notch.
I've polished my glasses, removed a small speck.
I've looked at my check stubs to check on a check,
I've searched for my tweezers and pulled out a hair,
I've opened a window to let in some air,
I've straightened a picture, I've swatted a fly,
I've shifted the tie clip that clips down my tie,
I've sharpened each pencil till sharp as a dirk...
I've run out of reasons for not starting work.

Richard Armour[1]

Every day each of us receives a special gift, a gift of 1440 parts. These are the minutes of a new day, which God gives to us with regularity.

What a beautiful gift! Many things can be bought in the market. But time is not one of them. True, we can purchase what is accomplished during time, but time itself is strictly a gift of God.

Time has no favorites. We all have exactly the same amount of time as our neighbor. The question is, how do we use that time?

All of us are acquainted with individuals who seem to have the ability to multiply the value of time. Many of us remember parents, especially mothers, who had that gift. My father put in his full day seven days a week as a rose grower in a humid greenhouse, which left little time or energy for much else.

But Mother took care of her family almost incidentally to maintaining the household itself. For many years she also had a regular outside job, and, like everyone else in those days, sewed her own clothes. To top it off, there was the huge amount of canning that kept the immigrant Graendorf family in fruit and vegetables during the winter months.

How did these women do it? I don't think Mom ever had a work time study. But she surely knew how to use the available minutes.

Minutes. Maybe that was it. People who have learned to use time successfully are generally able to put minutes to work.

I like the story of the traveler in the Swiss Alps. As he traveled, he came one day to an Alpine valley containing two farms. The scene was picture-book lovely, and the traveler drank in the view.

The farms were opposite each other, and as the man enjoyed the scene he became increasingly aware that the two farms were quite different. The more he studied them, the more he saw that the one was in much better condition than the other. The house was bigger, neater. The barns were more substantial looking, and the equipment was in better repair.

There was even a difference in the way the two owners worked. The traveler could see the one man moving about in great agitation. He seemed to be under considerable pressure to get his work done.

By contrast, the other farmer, the redhead who had the nicer farm, worked steadily and calmly. In fact, the way the second man worked seemed much more appropriate to the whole Alpine scene, and the traveler observed it all in fascination.

Finally, the traveler's curiosity got the better of him.

Approaching the redhead directly, he asked if there was a reason for the obvious contrast in the two farms.

"Oh, quite simple," the ruddy-faced farmer replied as he pulled contemplatively on his mountaineer's pipe. "When I first came to the mountains I observed another man building here, and I decided to learn from him. I soon discovered that he was using only big, beautiful rocks — hard to find and difficult to handle. At the end of the day he usually complained bitterly on the lack of usable rocks and the general difficulty of building. It was discouraging work, and often I noticed that he stopped working for several days.

"Anyhow," continued the ruddy farmer, "I determined then to build my house with what was available and use small rocks as well as short minutes to get my work done. My neighbor continues to use only big pieces of rocks and time."

Therein, I think, also lies the secret of efficient people — they have learned to make use of the minutes that others often literally "let slip down the cracks."

The principle is simple. Put to work the minute that you actually have, rather than waiting for the hour that may or may not become available.

This type of time management has three simple steps: (1) Make a listing of time available — large, small, regular or occasional — by minutes (e.g., 10:00 - 10:30 A.M.; 2:00 - 2:15 P.M.; 4:00 - 5:00 P.M., *each day*). (2) Keep a listing of work or projects to be done that day (e.g., pay bills; write sister; clean front windows). (3) Assign work to a specific time from the time list (e.g. 10:00 - 10:30, write sister). Use a simple priority system (A = top priority; B = secondary importance; C = when all else is completed) to give each project a priority listing.

Each person can set up his own system, but these are the basics. You need to get the task and the work time together. Depending upon your own artistic nature, your record keeping can be as detailed or as simple as you wish. For many years I used a plain 3" X 5" index card to record my daily personal task assignments. This worked fine for my purpose. I just put it in my pocket date book. I made out a new card each afternoon for the next day and checked off each assignment when completed.

The recommendation is to strive for simplicity. When I first began teaching I had developed a very fancy system for keeping personal records. One day a colleague of mine observed me struggling with my intricate system. Finally he said quietly, "I'm sure that's a great system you've got there, Graendorf. But explain to me what it actually accomplishes." That is when I quietly changed to the index card!

This reminds me of the junior high teacher who loved to impress his students with statistics. One day be became intrigued with world death rates and proceeded to give a dramatic presentation to his class. As he came to the climax, the teacher pointed to a student on the front row and proclaimed, "Why, each time Edward there takes a breath, three people in the United States die. What do you think of that?" He waited for an awed response.

From the back row came the deflating answer: "Tell him about Scope!"

The time management consultant, Alan Lakein, writes movingly in his book, *How to Get Control of Your*

Time and Life, on the importance of controlling our time: "Time is life. It is irreversible and irreplaceable. To waste your time is to waste your life, but to master your time is to master your life and make the most of it."[2]

While we may insist that we are, as Ernest Henley wrote, "the masters of our fate," we are to a great extent manipulated by circumstances.

The older adult is less and less inclined to direct his ongoing activities aggressively. An increasingly common expression becomes, "What ever happened to yesterday?" As life often becomes a succession of predetermined events, it loses much of its zest.

Lakein offers some basic suggestions. Primary among these is to define lifetime goals. That is, determine what you really want from life (see chapter 8, "Reason for Living"). Writing down some basic goals serves to provide overall direction for the use of time.

Lakein combines this direction with a *to-do list* and a *schedule.* As you'll observe, this follows a pattern similar to the 1-2-3 step approach, for time control.

Finally, Lakein adds the Lakein Question. This is simply asking, "What is the best use of my time right now?" The point is to be as productive as possible because you are definitely doing what is of value to you.

A crucial factor in any effective time planning, of course, is the written memo. As we get older, most of us benefit considerably from visual reminders.

Beyond the general use of time is the Christian perspective. For one thing, God's daily gift of 1440 minutes is preparation time for eternity. How to use it well is our ongoing daily challenge, as we gratefully appropriate the daily cleansing noted in 1 John 1:7.

Perhaps one of the most accomplished individuals mentioned in the Bible was David — poet, athlete, soldier, general, musician, statesman, king. He certainly had to use his 1440 minutes wisely each day; and I think he shared his secret of success in Psalm 31:15, NIV: "My times are in your hands." Clearly, he daily dedicated his time to the Lord.

Again, one of the greatest incentives for such dedication of time is the recognition that these God-given hours are our investment for eternity.

How do we evaluate the length of eternity? I have always enjoyed Henrick Van Loon's illustration with which he began his *Story of Mankind.*

"Suppose," he wrote, "that we have a high rock in the far North Country — it is a hundred miles high and a hundred miles wide. Once every thousand years a little bird comes to this rock to sharpen its beak.

When that rock has thus been worn away, then a single day of eternity will have gone by."

Happy indeed is the person who finds a good balance in his use of time. We are people of various parts, and there is a legitimate use for a variety of activity. There is, for example, a place for social and physical activity as well as relaxation. Our Lord recognized this when he watched his own disciples become so busy in His service that they had no time to eat.

So we have the Master's own words: "Come with me by yourselves to a quiet place and get some rest" (Mark 6:31, NIV). What a remarkable affirmation for the balanced use of time!

In his fine little volume on *How to Save Time in the Ministry,* my friend Les Flynn has this verse:

> I have only just a minute
> Just sixty seconds in it;
> Forced upon me — can't refuse it.
> Didn't seek it, didn't choose it.
> I must suffer if I lose it,
> Give account if I abuse it.
> Just a tiny little minute,
> But eternity is in it.[3]

Says a lot.

I have found Engstrom and Mackenzie's study, *Managing Your Time,* especially helpful. In it the authors point out that management of time for the Christian is actually management of *His* time.

If this is so, then ". . . when times get out of joint . . . when tasks pile up . . . and when things go wrong . . . how often do we stop to ask God if we're doing what *He* wants us to do? It is *His* time we're managing; isn't *this* where we should begin?"[4]

Suggestions for Enriching Your Study

The Christian's use of time has challenging implications both for the present and for eternity.

(a) Read Ephesians 5:15-17 in several translations.

(b) Do a little study on how much of an average day in your life you could consider to be of eternal value. How could you sharpen it up?

(c) Write out several ideas on making better use of your time by using minutes.

UNIT FOUR

Compatible Aging

UNIT FOUR
Compatible Aging . . .

Jesus grew . . . in favor . . . with men (Luke 2:52, NIV).
Live in harmony, (Philippians 4:2).

The older I get, the more I realize that I can get along well with everybody except people.

The fourth key for successful aging (following Jesus' pattern of personal development in Luke 2) concerns our relationship with people. How well do we get along with others — spouse, family, neighbors, friends, associates? As we become older, the answer to that question increasingly indicates how well we really enjoy life.

Compatible contact can provide us with some of the most satisfying experiences of our older adult lives. Yet paradoxically, relationships with others can also be the source of intense misery. Thus, a key concern in older adult happiness is knowing how to get along well with others, which is the focus of this unit.

It begins with *people relationships in general.* What, basically, makes for living in harmony with others? How do we achieve it?

Another chapter focuses on the ultimate partnership of men and women — *marriage* — still the most significant continuing relationship for the older adult. What are some of the keys?

The final chapter in the unit considers the consummate relationship — the *family of God.* Believers are joined in unique fellowship as brothers and sisters in Christ, which in its visible form is identified as a church, a body of people whose common destination is heaven.

While for many individuals life focuses on the present, for the believer the emphasis is, praise God, on looking ahead!

Chapter Eleven

COMPANIONSHIP

Do you still remember some of the "magic" terms of your younger days — words with significance quite beyond their normal meaning?

I'm sure we all have had them — terms like "Good Humor man," "family picnic," "Grandma's place," "summer vacation," and maybe even "old swimming hole." Magic words. For many of us, these words still evoke wonderfully nostalgic feelings.

From my own childhood there is a word that will always stand out. It is the simple term "company." For an only child in an immigrant family, "company" had natural magic. In fact, the word was able to transform this country lad into an alert, clean, well-mannered boy in a matter of minutes. Believe me, that's magic!

"Company" usually meant special people. When company was my favorite uncle, it normally also meant another copy of a Tom Swift (or was it Don Sturdy?) adventure book, a real treat. The focus, however, always remained on Uncle Paul and the opportunity to spend some time with him. And this was true whenever we had company. We enjoyed the opportunity to be with people.

Now as an older adult, I have again become aware of the rewarding place of people in my life. And that is natural. As Spinoza, the Dutch philosopher, once noted, man is a social animal. He interacts with others. Further, we need others, and companionship fills an important place in each person's life.

As John Donne, the 16th century English poet, expressed it so well, no man is an island, ". . . every man is a piece of the continent, a part of the main . . . any man's death diminishes me, because I am involved in mankind."

The ground of this goes back to Genesis, where the earliest history of man records that God said it was not good for the man to be alone (Genesis 2:18). Accordingly, God initiated companionship for Adam by the creation of Eve. In its broadest sense this was friendship, a close relationship between two people with a common interest.

But God also initiated the partnership of man and woman, or marriage, which in its intimate aspects provides for human propagation as well as companionship.

Companionship, which like the term it derives from, company, has the feeling of warmth. Both terms come from the Latin base of *com* (with) and *pan* (bread) — literally, sharing bread. Here is the thought of being with a person on a meal basis — being friendly enough, if you will, to have a congenial cup of coffee with someone.

One writer has defined companionship as two people enjoying sharing a narrow path together. I like that. Although it applies preeminently to marriage, it has meaning for all of us — including singles and those who may have lost a spouse. The circumstances differ, but the need for companionship is universal.

We are all human, and the human heart responds to others. In marriage, the companionship of husband

and wife matures into the comfortable relationship that comes with the passage of time.

But life is carried on with broader people contact — the butcher, the baker, family, neighbors, fellow workers — people with whom ongoing contact can be an enjoyable experience.

It is significant that Jesus got along well with people ("developed in favor with men"). The account in Luke 4 of His early activity notes that as He began His public ministry He was "praised [respected] by all" (verse 15), and "all were speaking well of Him" (verse 22). How did He do this? Let's examine some basics of good people relationships.

First of all, getting along well with people is a two-way street. The writer of the book of Proverbs has expressed it simply: "A man that hath friends must shew himself friendly" (18:24, KJV).

"My neighbors," complained Maria, "are very unfriendly." One day during strawberry season we asked Maria, who had an extensive strawberry patch, how often she shared her berries with neighbors. "Oh," was her reply, "not until they become more friendly."

Our farmer friend used to say, "It's a lot easier to make friends with a purring kitten than with a taciturn porcupine!"

For several years I shared with my Bible school students some of the practical suggestions given by a Missouri farm lad for getting along with people. They were good suggestions — so good, in fact, that the book he wrote in 1936 became the most popular non-fiction volume of the time. When as a college freshman I first bought a copy, it had stamped on it "copy number 2,050,742."

Do you recognize the book? You've probably seen it. It is Dale Carnegie's *How to Win Friends and Influence People*, and it contains a wealth of common-sense suggestions on the subject. Let's note six major thoughts:[1]

(a) *Become genuinely interested in other people.* In a materialistic society, we all respond to someone interested in us for our own sake.

(b) *Be a good listener.* It is interesting to realize the price people are willing to pay someone to listen to them. Listening, in fact, is the single most important ingredient in good counseling. It is easy to tell people what to do, but quite something else to let them express their own feelings.

(c) *Don't argue.* We have a natural tendency to be combative. Most of us have an inbred feeling of our rightness. But you never really win an argument, says Carnegie, and illustrates it with this bit of verse:

> Here lies the body of William Jay,
> Who died maintaining the right of way —
> He was right, dead right, as he sped along,
> But he's just as dead as if he were wrong.[2]

(d) *Learn to smile.* The world is full of sour notes. Happy is the person who has learned to bring cheerfulness into life. He is always well received!

(e) *Show appreciation.* Have you been fortunate enough to know people with a gracious spirit, for whom it is difficult not to do things? I think of a couple who exercised so neatly this gift of appreciation. Everyone was glad to count the Garners as their friends. They never forgot the word or note of thanks, no matter how small the deed. What beautiful friends they were!

(f) *Take initiative.* It is easy to wait for someone else to make the first move, and as a result it often never gets made. I like the way Edwin Markham expressed it in his poem, "Outwitted:"

> He drew a circle that shut me out —
> Heretic, rebel, a thing to flout,
> But Love and I had the wit to win:
> We drew a circle that took him in!

Desire to get along well with people! Put these suggestions into practice. They are tested principles.

There is another consideration. As I chatted one day with a teaching colleague about Carnegie's principles, he casually asked if I realized where Carnegie got many of his ideas, and proceeded to point out their origin in biblical principles. And he was right.

For example, a major Carnegie principle is to be interested in the other person. He states it as "Talk in terms of the other person's interest."[3] Here was a principle that the writer Paul had expressed nearly two thousand years earlier when he wrote a letter to a group of Christians in the city of Philippi: "Each of you should look not only to your own interests, but also to the interests of others" (Philippians 2:4, NIV).

But Paul had also added that we had a model to guide us in this: "Your attitude should be the same as that of Christ Jesus" (Philippians 2:5, NIV). And this attitude in terms of respecting the interests of others is a clue to Paul's ability to get along with people.

Carnegie also stresses the value of remembering names. He suggests that a person's name represents to that person "the sweetest and most important sound in any language."[4]

It is said that one of Franklin D. Roosevelt's secrets as a successful politician was his ability to remember the name of each person he met.

Making an effort to remember names is not only of value to a politician, but is a valuable asset for anyone seeking to improve his relationship with others. The life of Christ provides an example. When Andrew brought his brother to meet Jesus, the Lord greeted Peter by using his name. "'You are Simon the son of John,' He said" (John 1:42).

Likewise, He addressed Martha personally in the confrontation with Mary (Luke 10:41) and Judas in the betrayal scene (Luke 22:48), as well as Zaccheus in the sycamore tree (Luke 19:5).

A final suggestion on getting along with people is from A. Donald Bell's *How to Get Along With People in the Church.* He begins his interesting book with the note that ninety percent of all working people who fail in their life's vocation fail because they cannot get along with people.[5]

One of Bell's primary recommendations is to be open-minded when you meet people. It is risky to stereotype individuals.

And, of course, the basic guideline for working well with people remains the venerated words of Christ Himself from Matthew 7:12 (Phillips), "Treat other people exactly as you would like to be treated by them . . ."

Suggestions for Enriching Your Study

Getting along well with others is important at any stage in life. It has special significance as we seek to avoid being characterized as "crotchety oldsters."

(a) Review some "magic" words from your own background.

(b) What do you consider your most helpful assets for getting along well with people? Biggest problems to work at?

(c) Choose three of the six Carnegie principles from the chapter that you feel will be of most help to you for improving your relationship with people and practice them for a week.

Chapter Twelve

PARTNERSHIP

"I married my Joe," says Emma of her fussing, recently retired husband, "for better or for worse, but not for lunch!"

That may sound like simply a clever expression, but for a couple struggling with older adult adjustments, it's no joke.

As it is being said more and more in these days of marriage tension, marriage that at one time was routinely identified as partnership has now too often become a matrimonial sinking ship.

There is an excellent reason for using the term partnership for describing marriage. Let me give an example. Anticipating getting involved in a business relationship, I once checked out specifically what it meant to set up a partnership. It is, explained the business dictionary I consulted, *a contractual agreement of joint rights and responsibilities for the purpose of establishing a mutually beneficial venture.*

What a neat working definition for marriage!

"Joint rights" — as a business partner I could expect to use the equipment and assets that the venture holds for the partners. As a marriage partner, the home and properties, as well as such matters as conjugal rights, are "ours." Effective marriage is a shared operation.

Not only is it a matter of shared rights, it is also, as in a business partnership, a matter of shared responsibilities, with both partners working together for mutual benefits.

I recently came across the copy of a letter sent by Benjamin Franklin, advising a friend about getting married. In it Franklin nicely emphasizes this matter of togetherness:

> It is the Man and Woman united that makes the complete human Being.
>   Separate she wants his force of Body and Strength and Reason; he her Softness, Sensibility and acute Discernment. Together they are most likely to succeed in the World. A single Man has not nearly the Value he would have in that State of Union. He is an incomplete Animal. He resembles the odd Half of a Pair of Scissors.
>   If you get a prudent, healthy wife, your Industry in your Profession, with her good Economy, will be a Fortune sufficient.[1]

This sharing relationship of husband and wife also finds a model in the biblical description of the church as a sharing body, as recorded in Acts 4:32 (NIV): "All the believers were one in heart and mind. No one claimed that any of his possessions was his own, but they shared everything they had."

Certainly one of the primary keys for a successful marriage is the recognition and sharing of common interests. In its simplest form, this is recognizing the give and take of living together, sharing in the physical, emotional, social and spiritual implications of living. For most of us this includes the realization that there is no "perfect" partnership.

My pastor, Chuck Swindoll, in his biblical study of marriage, *Strike the Original Match,* has this pertinent comment: "Christian marriages have conflicts, but they are not beyond solution. . . . *Remember this:* There is no such thing as a home completely without conflicts. The last couple to live 'happily ever after' was Snow White and Prince Charming."[2]

As Swindoll would add, perfect marriages require perfect people, and there just aren't too many of those around!

Accepting each other's human frailties and working at them together is a basic step to succeeding in marriage. Notice that it is not working at his or hers, but working together.

I remember the fine presenation by Lloyd Ogilvie, pastor of the First Presbyterian Church of Hollywood, given as part of the dramatic 1975 Continental Congress on the Family held in St. Louis. Referring to the principle of honesty in his own marriage, Ogilvie noted: ". . . I was able to surrender my efforts to remold my wife and begin to accept her as the very special and unique gift God had given me."[3]

Ogilvie suggested that *honesty* in the marriage relationship is a first key for successful marriage. "It is not," he emphasized, "just telling the truth. In marriage it is being open to the truth about ourselves." (Continental Congress on the Family notes)

In his chapter, "Commitment Is the Key," Swindoll adds another important key for a good marriage: *commitment.*

"Marriage," he reminds us, "isn't begun in a context of vagueness and uncertainty. Two people, fully conscious and very much awake and aware, declare their vows."[4]

He adds incisively:

> No amount of psychological therapy, positive thinking (often dubbed "grace"), semantic footwork with the biblical text, alternative concepts, or mutual support from family and friends can remove your responsibility to *keep your vow*.[5]

Swindoll suggests four helpful principles to help work out the understanding of marriage commitment, beginning with the already noted truth that Christian marriages have conflicts.

The second principle is that "working through is harder than walking out, but it is God's way."

Third: "Being committed to one's mate is not a matter of *demanding rights, but releasing rights.*"

Finally, there is the principle that "The Christian's ultimate goal in life is not to be happy, but to glorify God."[6]

A husband and wife team, Sally and Jim Conway, who have pioneered the current Christian approach to mid-life crisis, have produced some helpful counseling materials. Although originally focused on the crisis needs of husband or wife, the material has a wider application that fits well for mates of either gender.

This material from Sally's writing seems especially appropriate:

> Loving (your spouse) includes accepting him (her) as the person is at the moment . . . value without strings attached . . . unconditional love . . .

> Love grows by cultivation, by looking at the positive qualities of the one you love, by putting yourself out to meet needs.[7]

Implicit in the marriage counseling materials of such writers as Norman Wright is the principle of communication. The center of all good communication is the willingness to listen, and, as one writer has expressed it so well, not only with the ear, but, most importantly, with the heart. As a young Christian education director working on a graduate degree, I, with my wife, found it extremely helpful to establish a regular time for communication, such as an inviolable Friday night dinner date.

Becoming older has significant implications for marriage, both positive and negative. As we age we sometimes become less patient with our spouses, and health difficulties can make us irritable. On the other hand, the years can provide a welcome mellowness that, together with the comfortable association of years, makes living together more simple and pleasant.

That consummate literature on human relations, the thirteenth chapter of First Corinthians, offers ultimate guidance for the happiest partnership.

Listen to it again:

> Love is patient,
> Love is kind. . . .
> Is not rude,
> It is not self-seeking,
> It is not easily angered. . . .
> It always protects,
> Always trusts. . . .
> Love never fails.

(1 Cor. 13:4-8, NIV)

Suggestions for Enriching Your Study

A husband and wife face the challenge of working together to make older adult marriage a continuing delight.

(a) What strengths does a Christian approach bring to marriage?

(b) From your observation of other marriages, what do you sense to be two major difficulties? Consider some solutions.

(c) Would you consider that your parents' marriage
was easier or more difficult to maintain successfully than
yours? Why?

Chapter Thirteen

THE FAMILY OF GOD

It seems appropriate for a closing chapter on older adult living to focus on one of the most permanent of all relationships — the family of God, — and in the process take a truly happy look at aging!

We live in a world that Scottish hymn writer, Henry Lyte, described in his hymn, *Abide With Me,* with the words, "change and decay in all around I see."

But Lyte concluded that verse of his hymn with, "O thou who changest not, abide with me," reminding us that in the midst of life's uncertainties there can be Certainty (Hebrews 13:8).

We who are part of God's family indeed have a secure, everlasting relationship.

Edith Schaeffer, the widow of Francis Schaeffer,[1] has expressed it neatly in her book, *What Is A Family?* She writes:

> Happily, there *is* a Perfect Family, a completely "one" Family, and a home that is waiting for each member of that Family, where the environment will be without flaw

for all eternity . . . There is a home ahead, for each one
of the children of the Lord who have been born into His
Family. . . There *is* a Family — with a Heavenly Father.[2]

I like that — there is "a home ahead."

We have several ways of looking at life. For some it
is composed largely of memories. It is pleasant, of course,
to remember happy experiences. But where the focus of
life is mostly on what has gone on before, it is a bit like
yesterday's breakfast — interesting perhaps, but not very
nourishing.

But life can also be seen as purely the present, where
the only value is considered to be that which exists now.
Many accept this. It is the existentialist mode of the
"now" generation that lives for today. But this is like
breakfast in which any spark of anticipation has been
removed.

There is a third type of living, one that finds focus
in expectation. Each day is fresh with the wonderment
of what lies ahead. It is the "small boy exhilaration" for
a life full of a thoughtful Father's good things.

It is the exciting script that reads "In my Father's
house are many mansions . . . . I go to prepare a place
for you" (John 14:2, KJV).

What security for the Christian believer! We're reminded again of Dorothea Day's poem (Chapter 2) and
her contrast to William Henley's "horror of the shade"
with the words, "that life with Him....keeps and shall
keep me unafraid!"

There is here no frightening future for the child of
God, no specter of a "War of the Worlds."

"War of the Worlds." Do you remember it, the Orson
Welles radio program in 1938 that caused such a national
hysteria and probably one of the most frightening programs ever presented on public radio?

It still brings back macabre memories to me of that Sunday evening in October. I had been driven back to college that night after a weekend spent at home. What a wretched night! The fog that evening on the thirty-mile drive was horrendous as we progressed at a snail's pace, then stopped to assist some folks involved in a serious auto accident. When we arrived at my college dorm we learned from the shaken people on campus of the CBS broadcast that had dramatized the story of a Martian invasion.

The broadcast had been done so realistically that a later study indicated that at least one million of the six million who reportedly heard the broadcast actually believed an invasion had taken place!

(Looking back, I have wondered if that engulfing fog on our drive back to the campus, which provided such a dramatic setting for the broadcast report, wasn't part of Orson Welles's planning genius!)

But the panic that resulted all over the country that night was real. People got into their cars and left metropolitan areas in droves to escape the "invaders." The metal invasion cylinder had landed, it was reported, near Grovers Mill, New Jersey. Chaos in the eastern area was complete. As the grotesque reaction to the "Mercury Theater on the Air" production began to become known, the CBS producers sent out correction news bulletins to calm the rising panic, but to little avail.

Among the results of that memorable evening was the making of the reputation of 23-year-old-actor/producer Orson Welles. It also, of course, demonstrated the awesome power of imaginative suggestion.

But for me, as a young Christian collegian, the traumatic episode that night served to indelibly reinforce my appreciation for the overshadowing presence of God. How reassuring it was that evening to reflect on the heavenly Father's care for His children!

Recently, one of my classmates from those college days, well known evangelist Billy Graham wrote similarly in *Decision* magazine, "I am an optimist because I know that when I die I will go into the presence of Christ."[3]

I was fortunate at the time to have a close association with V. Raymond Edman, who was to become the president of Wheaton College. Some years after college graduation when Marge and I were married, "prexy" presented us with a copy of his *Delights of Life,* which contains a fine chapter on "Destination," some notes in his own warm style on the topic of death. In his comments Edman remembers his bout on the mission field with typhus fever, which brought him close to death in Ecuador. As he recollects, "friend wife" had already dyed her wedding dress black in anticipation of a funeral service.

I've always appreciated his subsequent notes related to dying. He wrote:

> Death is an enemy, that is true. But it is a foe already defeated . . . God's trusting children need have no fear; and down the ages they have re-echoed David's sweet testimony: "Yea, though I walk through the valley of the shadow of death, I will fear no evil." (Psalm 23:4)
>
> Further, God's children have blessing while they live and when they die. They can live without fear of death, because their Lord has conquered it for them. From the Patriarch Job to the beloved Apostle John, there rings throughout the Bible a strong word of complete confidence and assurance.
>
> To die is gain . . . to be with Christ is far better! To the child of God, born again of God's Spirit and Word, death is not the end of life; rather, it is the "commencement" of life in eternity.[4]

This is the joyous future prospect of the members of the family of God! Meanwhile, participation in the life of the Christian family now is an ongoing blessing. As Edith Schaeffer writes:

. . . family loyalty is something the Bible points out as a mark of the Family of the Lord. When one part of the body hurts or is affected by something, the whole body is affected. This is the way it is meant to be in the "body of Christ" which is the Lord's Family made up of believers. . . The larger Family of the Lord is meant to take care of each other with a feeling for each other's hurts.[5]

Here is the beautiful picture of our Christian relationship as members of the body of Christ, as described in 1 Corinthians 12:12-27.

There is a lovely song called "The Family of God" that's been written by the Gaither family:

> I'm so glad I'm a part of the family of God —
> I've been washed in the fountain, cleansed by His blood!
> Joint heirs with Jesus as we travel this sod,
> For I'm part of the family, the family of God.[6]

As the well-known evangelist, James McGinley, would always conclude in his heavy Scotch burr, "Now isn't that just grand!"

Suggestions for Enriching Your Study

One of the exhilarating truths included in a Christian approach to aging is that it means being able to look forward to a glorious future.

(a) What are some characteristics of God as our heavenly Father?

(b) Make an effort to memorize John 14:1-4.

(c) What makes the family of God the most permanent of all relationships?

Conclusion

Chapter Fourteen

FOUR KEYS
AND AN AXIOM

These chapters were written to help you make the most out of your over-fifty years. Making the most could include longer life gained by applying some of the practical suggestions included. Fine. But good living must be evaluated as much by its *quality* as by its length. So our prime purpose is to guide you toward making your life's journey as enjoyable as possible. With that in mind, let's summarize better living at this stage of existence, as it has been presented in this book.

There are first the four keys based on the pattern of Christ's life, as recorded for us by the physician-writer Luke in the Bible (Luke 2:52).

Keys, as you know, are used to open doors. In this case the door which is being opened is more effective living and the keys are what you and I can do to improve that living. Keys, remember, do not turn by themselves.

The first key is establishing (or reaffirming) a *spiritual perspective* on life, as laid out in the first three chapters. In its simplest expression, this means growing steadily in our understanding and appreciation of God as our creator, architect-planner and sustainer. Here is a basis for the happy flavor of confident living. Life can be positive. [A daily quiet time offers what is perhaps the best opportunity for accomplishing this. See the next chapter.]

A second key is to face life with *mental alertness.* As spelled out in the third unit this means productive (worthwhile) living through having purpose and goals in life.

The third key you can use is *good physical condition.* It involves keeping reasonably healthy by means of sound nutrition and practical exercise, as discussed in the second unit.

The last key is *social empathy* — getting along well with people. This is something in which we can all improve, and in so doing we will find ourselves also improving in our ability to cope with life.

Notice that we have four practical keys. To open doors, we must put keys to work. So spiritual perspective comes from having spiritual contact. Likewise, an alert mind is a mind that reads and thinks. Improved physical condition results from better eating and applied exercise. Getting along better with people is something that repays being worked at.

Successful living takes effort.

How much effort does it take? That's where the axiom — an established guideline — comes in. By combining the four keys (*P*erspective, *A*lertness, *C*ondition, *E*mpathy), their first letters spell out our axiom: *PACE.* At the heart of effective aging is the principle of learning to pace yourself.

By its very nature, growing older represents a change in our abilities. It does not mean *ceasing;* it does mean *adjusting.* I still enjoy recreational activities, but I no longer attempt the strenuous game of pickup basketball that I once delighted in. Marge still enjoys having guests over for dinner. But no big shindigs. We have learned to do things in moderation, to pace ourselves.

It is the principle spelled out for older adults in the Bible. Paul wrote in his epistles that folks who are older (Titus 2:2 — older men; I Timothy 3:11 — leaders' wives) are to learn to be temperate. The idea is to be in control, to use good judgment. It is the thought expressed in Philippians 4:5 by "moderation."

What practical advice. This axiom to pace ourselves suggests that we no longer need to give in to what in the past has often been pressure to produce or to keep up with appearances.

Pete Rose, the veteran baseball player/manager who remains outstanding in his field past the age of forty, has made the statement that he could still perform the skills for which he was noted over the years, but no longer every day.

Here is pacing — learning to recognize and understand our limitations. For some this may mean to slow down occasionally and do fewer demanding activities each day. For others it could be stopping for a while in order to regroup. No guilt feelings need be involved here.

In the aging process it is important to recognize when to slow down.

Perhaps it could be said that the older adult who pauses to stop and refresh along the way will be able to pick up and carry on another day (with apologies to Tertullian, the third century church leader who first expressed the feeling applied to combat).

Chapter Fifteen

COMPASS FOR CONFIDENT OLDER ADULT LIVING

Confident living, like confident traveling, benefits considerably from a dependable compass.

A compass provides direction to keep us on the right track.

For example, the small metal and glass instrument hanging here on my study wall began as my father's army tool which guided him throughout Europe as an army scout in the first world war. It is thoroughly battle-tested and dependable. It continues to function well. A buddy and I put it to work a few years ago when we got lost on an exploration trip in the north woods of Michigan's upper peninsula. Got us home safely.

This is a magnetic compass, for when its compass needle is allowed to swing freely, it will accurately point to north. Thus it provides geographic direction to guide an individual to his destination.

Fortunate is the person who has such a useful instrument available when geographic direction is needed!

But what about a compass to provide direction for life, guidance for meaningful living?

Good news. Such guidance is also available!

I first became personally acquainted with it during my high school years when I was introduced, one summer day, to the reality of Christianity — and to the Guide.

My introducer was evangelist Gypsy Smith, and his platform for the gospel presentation that day was an old Majestic radio in our family living room.

At first the experience of becoming part of the Christian fellowship was so stimulating that it took me a while to comprehend that Christianity is considerably more than a one-time event. It is a process of living, an ongoing experience. And it has its ups and downs, as I found out.

As Christians develop, we need guidance. We need, indeed, what might be termed a compass — something that can provide direction for Christian living. Such direction can be found most directly in the New Testament. As an example, let's look at Christ's familiar story of the Father's house (heaven) in John 14:1-6.

"In my Father's house," Jesus began, "are many rooms."

And He continued, "You know the way to that place."

But then as part of the discussion, one of Christ's followers that day spoke up and said, in effect, "Sorry, we really don't know where You are going . . . or the direction" [way, path, road — the same word for direction is used in James 2:25, NIV].

It is here that we have one of the most remarkable pronouncements of all time.

"I," said Jesus in answering His disciple's uncertainty, "am your direction. You come to God through Me." (Meaningful living begins in establishing our relationship with God through Jesus Christ.)

What a striking thought — a person as direction!

No cold metal and glass instrument this. Here is a *living* guide, in effect a living compass. How significant, because one of the distinctives of Christianity is that its focus is a person, rather than a creed or philosophy.

Similarly, being a Christian is fundamentally a relationship, not an organization: "But as many as received Him, to them He gave the right to become children of God" (John 1:12); "Now this is eternal life: that they may know you, the only true God, and Jesus Christ, whom you have sent" (John 17:3, NIV).

Our guidance, then, is through contact with a personal God.

"I will guide thee," says this God in Psalm 32:8, (KJV) "with mine eye."

I like that. God is going to keep an eye on us.

One of the few wall plaques I have kept in my study has the words of Solomon in Proverbs 3:6 (KJV): "In all thy ways acknowledge him, and he shall direct thy paths."

He (God) will provide direction. In a world of uncertainty and confusing pathways, we are offered a personal guide!

And Solomon also gives the condition for getting that direction. It is simply that we are to acknowledge God (give Him recognition) in all our ways. The Living Bible translation has given this helpful paraphrase for the verse: "In everything you do, put God first."

And how does one do that, put Him first?

Drawing a page from courting days, I'd say the first essential would be to plan for meaningful communication. When I lived in a men's dormitory in college, it was relatively easy to spot the fellows with special friends back home. They were the ones who managed to be first to the mailboxes. That regular personal communication was vital!

Communication with God. First, the wonder of it.

We have in our day become increasingly casual about life, including its spiritual dimension. I was a bit startled recently, to hear an outstanding sports personality refer offhandedly on a television church program to the "big, blue Dodger in the sky!"

Perhaps I betray my liturgical upbringing, but I find it difficult to think of the creator of the universe in those terms. Now, understand that I have little sympathy with dignity that is confused with stuffiness. But I am convinced that true dignity has the atmosphere of majesty. Accordingly, I appreciate hymns like the great Swedish song of Carl Boberg, "How Great Thou Art," with its inspiring words:

> O Lord my God! when I in awesome wonder
> Consider all the worlds Thy hands have made,
> I see the stars, I hear the rolling thunder,
> Thy pow'r throughout the universe displayed . . .
> How great thou art![1]

The wonder of communication with God.

In effective interchange, there is always two-way communication. God has a message for me, and I respond to Him.

His word for me is identified, appropriately enough, as God's Word. These sixty-six volumes, collectively called the Bible, contain a fascinating array of material, ranging from the origin of the universe in Genesis to its consummation in the book of Revelation. In between is the wisdom (and wit, as in Proverbs) needed for successful living.

Here is one of the world's greatest pieces of literature. Some years ago in an old magazine I discovered a graphic discription of the Bible that has always impressed me. It was written by an unknown minister:

When I found the wonderful temple of Christianity, I entered at the portico of Genesis, walked through the Old Testament art galleries, where the pictures of Noah, Abraham, Isaac, Jacob, Joseph, Moses, and Daniel hung on the wall; I passed into the music hall of Psalms, where the spirit swept the keyboard of nature until it seemed that every reed and pipe of God's great organ responded to the tuneful harp of David, the sweet singer of Israel.

I entered the chamber of Ecclesiastes, where the voice of the preacher was heard; and into the conservatory of Sharon, and the Lily of the Valley's sweet-scented spices filled and perfumed my life.

I entered the business office of Proverbs, and then into the observatory room of the Prophets, where I saw telescopes of various sizes, pointing to far-off events, but all concentrated upon the bright and morning Star, which was above the moonlit hills of Judea for our salvation.

I entered the audience room of the King of kings, and caught a vision of His glory from the standpoint of Matthew, Mark, Luke and John; passed into the Acts of the Apostles, where the Holy Spirit was doing His work in the formation of the infant church. Then into the correspondence room, where sat Paul, Peter, James, and John, penning their epistles.

I stepped into the throne room of Revelation, where toward the glittering peaks, I got a vision of the King sitting upon the throne in all His glory, and I cried:

> All hail the pow'r of Jesus' name!
> Let Angels prostrate fall;
> Bring forth the royal diadem,
> and crown Him Lord of all!

The pages of this book, the Bible, contain God's direction (compass) for my life. Through reading and studying it, together with my communication with God in prayer, His direction becomes clarified for me.

Most of us have a relationship with God that finds somewhat regular expression in a weekly church service of some kind. It provides opportunity for corporate worship, teaching and fellowship — time with the people of God.

This is an important part of the normal Christian life. However, there is also strong scriptural encouragement for daily *individual* communication with God.

Thus the writer of Psalms notes in 88:9 (NIV), "I call to you, O Lord, every day." And again, there is the emphasis, "Every day I will praise you" (Psalm 145:2, NIV).

One of the most outstanding illustrations of the value of daily communication with God comes from the dramatic Old Testament story of the manna. This food, described as a wafer-like substance with a honey taste, was miraculously supplied by God each morning during Israel's forty years of wilderness wandering.

Aside from its remarkable supply, however, the distinctive feature of the manna was the day-by-day nature of its provision. The stipulation of the provision recorded in Exodus 16 was that the manna was to be gathered and used strictly on a daily basis (except for the Sabbath, for which an extra portion was to be gathered the previous day).

What a beautiful Old Testament lesson for us concerning regular communication with God! Like the original supply of manna, there is a fresh supply of God's blessing for us each day. We can claim it daily. And because our communication with the Lord is two-way, it includes the privilege of sharing with Him our daily cares and concerns.

Here is the basis for what is often identified as one-day-at-a-time living. For as we come to God each day, we increasingly learn to commit to, and leave with, the heavenly Father that day's direction, as well as its cares and stresses. Doing that consistently may not always be easy, but it offers the rich benefit of confident and meaningful living.

This is essentially what Jesus was teaching His disciples in Matthew 6:

> Therefore do not worry about tomorrow, for tomorrow
> will worry about itself. Each day has enough trouble
> of its own. (Matthew 6:34, NIV)

I first became acquainted with the "one day" emphasis for Christian living in an article written by Roger Voskuyl while he was president of Westmont College. Voskuyl, who had been my college physics prof, applied the principle to the gradual development of college students.

However, even more than with the article itself, I was struck by the inclusion of Annie Johnson Flint's moving poem, "One day at a Time." It is worth sharing:

> One day at a time, with its failures and fears,
> With its hurts and mistakes, with its weakness and tears,
> With its portion of pain and its burden of care;
> One day at a time we must meet and must bear. . . .
>
> Not yesterday's load we are called on to bear,
> Nor the morrow's uncertain and shadowy care;
> Why should we look forward or back with dismay?
> Our needs, as our mercies, are but for the day.
>
> One day at a time, and the day is His day;
> He hath numbered its hours, though they haste or delay.
> His grace is sufficient; we walk not alone;
> As the day, so the strength that He giveth His own.[2]

I like the reminder in this poem that the "one day" being considered is *His* (God's) day. There is confidence — trust — in the One who controls the day.

A child has such trust in its parents. The Christian has confidence in the heavenly Father, confidence that normally finds expression through two basic activities: (a) listening to God through the reading of His Word; and (b) talking with God in prayer.

(a) *Reading God's Word.* Here is guidance, our compass, for the daily journey. "Your word is a lamp to my feet and a light for my path. . . Direct my footsteps according to your word" (Psalm 119:105,133, NIV). The immediate emphasis of this reading is not Bible study, which is an opportunity and challenge of its own. The reading mentioned here is simply to let God speak to us through His Word. With that in mind, there are some simple suggestions for getting the most out of this time with your Bible. To aid in remembering the suggestions, we use the initials *SOS* (*help* for Bible reading):

S — Systematically a chapter each morning from a Bible book such as Psalms or the Gospel of John. "The entrance of your words gives light" (Psalm 119:130, NIV).

O — Open your reading by asking God for an open heart and mind to understand what you read. "Open my eyes that I may see wonderful things in your law [the Bible]" (Psalm 119:18, NIV).

S — Seek the "so what" of personal application for your life that day from what you read. "This book of the law [the Bible] . . . meditate on it . . . so that you may be careful to do everything written in it" (Joshua 1:8, NIV).

(b) *Praying.* Here we talk with God about the day. "Morning by morning I lay my requests before you" (Psalm 5:3, NIV). Here are some simple suggestions to help guide your prayer time. To aid in remembering them we use the initials *WIN* (*winning,* being successful in praying):

W — Begin your praying with *worship,* realizing that we are talking with God, our heavenly Father. So we come confessing any sin ("If we confess our sins, He is faithful and righteous to forgive us our sins," 1 John 1:9) and being thankful for blessings ("With thanksgiving let your requests be made known to God" Philippians 4:6).

I — Include *intercession* by bringing before the Father your family members, friends, missionaries, and others. "Brethern, pray for us" (1 Thessalonians 5:25).

N — Present your own *needs* as you commit to God all the concerns of that day "Cast all your anxiety on him because he cares for you" (1 Peter 5:7, NIV).

There are, of course, extensive further suggestions and resources for personal communication with God. Some of us have developed and use our own programs and patterns. But the purpose of the above notes is to suggest some tested patterns of the simple elements of personal time with God to encourage those not having such a quiet time or to provide means for evaluating what you do have.

This time with the heavenly Father, which is sometimes called morning watch, personal devotions or daily quiet time, is much more than a mechanical exercise. It is a means by which we older adults especially are able to keep a positive look at daily life and living.

It is using quality time.

That means facing the challenge of priorities — deciding what is important in our use of time. For some this creates no difficulty. My mother, for example, had a very simple approach to priorities — what had to be done, got done. If that included (and it did) time spent with the Lord, our family put the time aside. Ours was a confident family.

But just how much time do you allow for communication with the Lord? Is there any specified amount? I
have never seen an authoritative answer, but I have
always appreciated my old friend Peter's comment when
asked about his devotional time. "I don't know about
you," he would say, "but I surely want to be well enough
acquainted with the Lord so I don't need any introduction
at the last minute!"

I feel more specific, perhaps, on the time of day
than I do on the amount of time (Psalm 5:3). Somehow,
the thought of "beginning the day with God" has fit
naturally into my family heritage. Early in my Christian
experience, Mother tucked the poem "The Secret" into
my Bible, with lasting impression:

> I met God in the morning
>   When the day was at its best,
> And His presence came like sunrise
>   With glory in my breast.
>
> All day long His presence lingered,
>   All day long He stayed with me,
> And we sailed with perfect calmness
>   O'er a very troubled sea.
>
> Other ships were blown and battered,
>   Other ships were sore distressed,
> But the winds that seemed to drive them
>   Brought to us both peace and rest.
>
> So, I think I know the secret,
>   Learned from many a troubled way —
> You must meet Him in the morning,
>   If you want Him through the day.[3]

There it is, devotions, quiet time, communication with
God — call it what you will. It represents the Christian's
regular personal contact with the Lord, our compass for
confident living.

Here is the spiritual foundation for making every
day count. The regular committing of the day to the

Father may not guarantee life without difficulties, but it certainly goes a long way toward providing God's peace for troubled times!

The Jerusalem Bible translation of 1 Peter 5:7 expresses well, I think, the warmth of that personal relationship with God: "Unload all your worries on to Him, since He is looking after you." We are talking about a *personal* relationship. God deals with me as an individual. Isn't that great?

The Lord understands me as I am, with my uniqueness and idiosyncracies. I need not fit into someone else's mold. This is certainly true of my communication time with the Lord. My prayers can be as simple and direct as I wish, for I am talking with my heavenly Father, person to person.

I need no knowledge of the original Bible languages of Greek and Hebrew to hear God's word for me.

As noted, many of us have our own approach to the details of personal devotional time. On the other hand, we can benefit from the suggestions and experiences of others. Thus there is the *SOS* pattern for Bible reading and the *WIN* guide for prayer.

Regardless of how you use it, put your "compass for confident aging" to work!

NOTES

Before You Begin
1. Douglas Kimmel, *Adulthood and Aging* (New York: Wiley & Sons, 1974), p. 345.

Chapter One
1. J. Oswald Sanders, *Your Best Years* (Chicago: Moody Press, 1982), p. 11.
2. U. S. Census Bureau, 1979.
3. Lilliam Dangott and Richard A. Kalish, *A Time to Enjoy* (New York: Prentice-Hall, 1979), p. 7.
4. Peter Mustric, *The Joy of Growing Older* (Wheaton, IL: Tyndale House, 1979).
5. Edgar Guest, "It Couldn't Be Done" from *Collected Verse of Edgar A. Guest* (Chicago: Contemporary Books, 1934), p. 285.

Chapter Two
1. Good reading here is J. Oswald Sanders, *Your Best Years* (Chicago: Moody Press, 1982) and Sam C. Reeves, *The Bright Years* (Old Tappan, NJ: Fleming H. Revell Company, 1977).
2. William Ernest Henley, "Invictus," *It Can Be Done,* comp. J. Morris (New York: George Sully & Company, 1921).
3. Dorothea Day, "My Captain," *Best Loved Poems* (New York: Doubleday & Company, 1936).

Chapter Three
1. K. Warner Schaie and James Geiwitz, *Adult Development and Aging* (Boston: Little, Brown and Co., 1982), p. 258.
2. Robert Butler, *Why Survive?* (New York: Harper & Row, 1975), p. 2.
3. J. Oswald Sanders, *Your Best Years* (Chicago: Moody Press, 1982), p. 19.
4. Tilman Smith, *In Favor of Growing Older* (Scottdale, PA: Herald Press, 1981), p. 67.
5. Jon Hendricks and C. Davis Hendricks, *Aging in Mass Society* (Cambridge, MA: Winthrop Publishers, Inc., 1981), p. 25.
6. Douglas Kimmel, *Adulthood and Aging* (New York: Wiley & Sons, 1974), p. 350.
7. Helen Hayes, *Our Best Years* (New York: Doubleday, 1984), p. 36.
8. Sam Levenson, *Everything But Money* (New York: Simon & Schuster, 1966), p. 12.
9. Ibid., p. 15.
10. Ibid., p. 16.
11. Ibid., p. 8.
12. Alexis Carrel, *Man the Unknown* (New York: Macfadden Books, 1939), p. 77.
13. Alfred Heller, *Your Body, His Temple* (Nashville: Thomas Nelson Publishers, 1981), p. 26.
14. Buster Crabbe, *Arthritis Exercise Book* (New York: Simon & Schuster, 1980).

15. Schaie, *Adult Development,* p. 236.
16. Ibid., p. 331.
17. Richard A. Kalish, *Late Adulthood: Perspectives on Human Development,* second ed. (Monterey, CA: Brooks, Cole Pub., 1982), p. 114.
18. Butler, *Why Survive?* p. 418.

Unit Two
1. Izaak Walton, *The Compleat Angler* (New York: Random House, n.d.), p. 288.
2. President's Council on Physical Fitness, *Adult Physical Fitness* (Washington, D.C.: U.S. Government Printing Office, n.d.), p. 5.
3. Margaret Heckler, in *Better Life Guide* (No. 1 of Campbell Soup's Series on Fitness, Box 4165, Chester, PA 19016).
4. The American Medical Association, *Family Medical Guide* (New York: Random House, 1982), p. 12.

Chapter Four
1. *Eat Better, Live Better* (Pleasantville, NY: Reader's Digest, 1982), p. 320.
2. Charles Kuntzleman, *Rating the Exercises* (New York: William Morrow, 1978), p. 19.
3. Jeffery Kunz, *American Medical Association Family Medical Guide* (New York: Random House, 1982), p. 15.
4. Ibid.
5. Herbert deVries and Dianne Hales, *Fitness After Fifty: An Exercise Prescription for Lifelong Health* (New York: Charles Scribner's Sons, 1982) p. 48.
6. Jane Brody, *Jane Brody's Nutrition Book* (New York: Bantam Books, 1981), n.p.
7. *Eat Better,* p. 320.
8. Magda Rosenberg, *Sixty-Plus and Fit Again* (New York: M. Evans, 1977), n.p.
9. David Stonecypher, "Law of Aging," *Getting Older and Staying Young* (New York: W. W. Norton & Co., 1974), p. 27.
10. Kunz, *Medical Guide,* p. 15.
11. *Eat Better,* p. 321.
12. Kuntzleman, *Rating,* p. 15.
13. Albert Marchetti, *Walking Book* (New York: Stein & Day, 1980), p. 12.
14. President's Council on Physical Fitness, *Adult Physical Fitness* (Washington, D.C.: U.S. Government Printing Office, n.d.), p. 64.
15. Kenneth Cooper, *New Aerobics* (New York: Evans & Co., 1970), p. 15.
16. Ibid.
17. Bob Anderson, *Stretching* (New York: Random House, 1980). p. 9.
18. *Eat Better,* p. 321.

19. Alfred L. Heller, *Your Body His Temple* (Nashville: Thomas Nelson, 1981), chapter 2.

Chapter Five
1. Robert M. Butler, quoted by Jane Brody, *Jane Brody's Nutrition Book* (New York: Bantam Books, 1981), p. 407.
2. Ibid., p. 408.
3. Ibid., p. 6.
4. Ibid.
5. Issued jointly by the U. S. Departments of Agriculture and Health and Human Services, 1980.
6. According to *Eat Better, Live Better* (Pleasantville, NY; Reader's Digest Association, 1982), this report notes possible impairment of mental and physical processes, and of vitamin and mineral deficiencies.
7. Chart adapted from *Nutrition: A Lifelong Commitment* by Juliet Bringas.
8. John A. Mann, *Secrets of Life Extension* (New York: Bantam Books, 1980), chapter 6.
9. Adapted from "Meal Planning for the Elderly," Reader's Digest, *Eating for Good Health.* (Also in *Eat Better, Live Better.*)
10. *Eat Better,* p. 282.
11. Ibid.
12. Cf. Alfred Heller, *Your Body His Temple* (Nashville: Thomas Nelson Publishers, 1981), chapter 16. See also Rose Dosti's helpful article, "Winning the Weight-Loss Game" in the *Los Angeles Times,* April 12, 1984.
13. Durk Pearson and Sandy Shaw, *Life Extension* (New York: Warner Books, 1982), p. 369.
14. Heller, *Your Body,* p. 171.

Chapter Six
1. J. J. Kramer, *Mobile Home Guide*
2. AIM Retirement Planning, "Housing and Location," 1978, p. 3.
3. Hubert Pryor, *Your Retirement Housing Guide* (Long Beach: AARP, 1975), p. 4.
4. Robert Havighurst, *Development Tasks and Education* (New York: David McKay Co., 1948), p. 96.
5. Joseph Michaels, *Prime of Your Life* (Boston: Little, Brown & Co., 1983), p. 201.

Chapter Seven
1. Bruce Larson, *There's a Lot More to Health Than Not Being Sick* (Waco, TX: Word, 1981), p. 143-44.
2. K. Warner Schaie and James Geiwitz, *Adult Development and Aging* (Boston: Little, Brown and Co., 1982), p. 260.
3. Ibid.

4. Retirement Advisors booklet, *Activities: How to Enjoy Leisure* (New York: Retirement Advisors, 1975), p. 3.
5. Mortimer Adler, *How to Read a Book* (Nashville, Convention Press, 1959).
6. Edmund Jacobson, *You Must Relax,* revised (New York: McGraw Hill/Whittlesey House, 1934).

Chapter Eight
1. Edward Dayton and Ted Engstrom, *Strategy for Living* (Glendale, CA: Regal Books, 1976), pp. 38,56,59.

Chapter Nine
1. Abraham Maslow, *Motivation and Personality* (New York: Harper and Row, 1970), en loco.
2. Paul Tournier, *Learn to Grow Old* (New York: Harper and Row, 1971), p. 117-18.
3. Joni Eareckson, *Joni* (Grand Rapids: Zondervan, 1975).

Chapter Ten
1. From a lecture presented at student chapel, Moody Bible Institute, March 11, 1968.
2. Alan Lakein, *How to Get Control of Your Time and Your Life* (New York: New American Library, 1973). p. 11.
3. Leslie Flynn, *How to Save Time in the Ministry* (Grand Rapids: Baker Book House, 1966). p. 14.
4. Ted Engstrom and Alec Mackenzie, *Managing Your Time* (Grand Rapids: Zondervan, 1967), p. 24.

Chapter Eleven
1. Dale Carnegie, *How to Win Friends and Influence People* (New York: Simon and Schuster, 1936).
2. Ibid., p. 135.
3. Ibid., p. 114.
4. Ibid., p. 100.
5. A. Donald Bell, *How to Get Along With People in the Church* (Grand Rapids: Zondervan, 1960), p. 11.

Chapter Twelve
1. David Legerman, ed., *Family Reading Book* (Garden City, NY: Doubleday and Co., 1952), p. 256.
2. Charles R. Swindoll, *Strike the Original Match* (Portland, Multnomah Press, 1980), p. 160.
3. Lloyd Ogilvie, "Marriage As It Was Meant to Be" (Notes: Continental Congress on the Family, 1975), p. 11.
4. Swindoll, *Original Match,* p. 152.
5. Ibid., p. 153.

6. Ibid., p. 164.
7. Sally Conway, *You and Your Husband's Mid-Life Crisis* (Elgin, IL: David C. Cook Pub., 1980), p. 189.

Chapter Thirteen
1. Francis Schaeffer was the world-renowned evangelical thinker and author, and with his wife was leader of the L'Abri Fellowship.
2. Edith Schaeffer, *What Is a Family?* (Old Tappan, NJ: Revell, 1975), p. 108.
3. Billy Graham, "Seven Lessons For Us," *Decision* (September 1985), vol. 26, no. 9, p. 1.
4. V. Raymond Edman, "Destination," *The Delights of Life* (Wheaton, IL: VanKampen Press, 1954), pp. 153-55.
5. Schaeffer, *Family*, p. 108.
6. "The Family of God," © William Gaither, *Hymns for the Family of God* (Alexandria, IN: Gaither Music Co., 1976). Used by permission.

Chapter Fifteen
1. Stuart K. Hine (Swedish, Carl Boberg), "How Great Thou Art," © 1953, renewed 1981, by Manna Music, Inc., 2111 Kenmere Ave., Burbank, CA 91504. International copyright secured. All rights reserved. Used by permission.
2. Annie Johnson Flint, "One Day at a Time," Westmont Courier (Church bulletin) (January/February 1957), vol.2, no. 3.
3. Ralph Cushman, "The Secret," *212 Victory Poems*, ed. Clifford Lewis (Grand Rapids: Zondervan, 1941).

ANNOTATED BIBLIOGRAPHY

Chapter Two

Dobbins, Gaines S. *The Years Ahead*. (Nashville: Convention Press, 1959.) A Southern Baptist study course, with well presented insights on aging.

Gray, Robert and Moberg, David. *The Church and the Older Person*. (Grand Rapids: Eerdmans, 1977.) One of the best studies on the religious focus of aging, with emphasis on church relationships.

Mustric, Peter. *The Joy of Growing Older*. (Wheaton: Tyndale, 1979.) Some practical observations, written by a church minister to senior citizens.

Ortland, Ray and Anne. *The Best Half of Life*. (Glendale, CA: Regal, 1976.) An informal discussion-type series of chats on aging by a minister and his wife.

Sanders, J. Oswald. *Your Best Years*. (Chicago: Moody Press, 1982.) A helpful series of chapters on aging that combine realism and optimism, by the octogenarian former director of OMF.

Stagg, Frank. *The Bible Speaks on Aging*. (Nashville: Broadman, 1981.) A good study on Bible teaching on aging by a retired seminary professor.

Tournier, Paul. *Learn to Grow Old*. (New York: Harper & Row, 1971.) A classic on aging by the famed Swiss doctor-psychologist.

Chapter Three

Butler, Robert N., M.D. *Why Survive? Being Old in America*. (New York: Harper & Row, 1975.) One of the pioneering studies on aging, heavily documented, with a solid whack at aging myths.

Clements, William M. (ed.) *Ministry with the Aging*. (New York: Harper & Row, 1981.) Aging concerns with a religious focus. Good material.

Hayes, Helen. *Our Best Years*. (New York: Doubleday, 1984.) A book of personal reflections from the 83-year-old first lady of the American theater, with commentaries on some two dozen older acquaintances, mostly from the entertainment field.

Hendricks, Jon and Hendricks, C. Davis. *Aging in Mass Society.* Second edition. (Cambridge: Winthrop Publishers, Inc., 1981). A sound textbook on the subject.

Kalish, Richard A. *Late Adulthood: Perspectives on Human Development.* Second edition. (Monterey, CA: Brooks/Cole Publishing Company, 1982.) A compact but thorough text on older adults.

Levenson, Sam. *Everything But Money.* (New York: Simon and Schuster, 1966.) A delightful book on the life of the Levenson family as they grew up in New York's East Harlem. A witty look at making the most out of limited circumstances.

Schaie, K. Warner and Geiwitz, James. *Adult Development and Aging.* (Boston: Little, Brown and Company, 1982.) Well written, contemporary material, nicely illustrated.

Smith, R. Tilman. *In Favor of Growing Older.* (Scottdale, PA: Herald Press, 1981.) A church-oriented study of the aging process with good resource material.

Chapter Four

Anderson, Bob. *Stretching.* (New York: Random House, 1980.) Sometimes referred to as flexing, this is a thorough study of this type of exercise. It is extensively illustrated.

Chandler, E. Ted. *How to Have Good Health.* (Nashville: Broadman, 1982.) A Christian perspective on health.

Cooper, Kenneth. *The New Aerobics.* (New York: Evans & Co., 1970.) This and the original *Aerobics* are the definitive books on the subject.

Gardner, Joseph. *Eat Better, Live Better.* (New York: Reader's Digest, 1982.) Called a "Commonsense Guide to Nutrition and Good Health," this has excellent nutritional material, with a good section on physical fitness.

Heller, A. L. *Your Body, His Temple.* (Nashville: Thomas Nelson Publishers, 1981.) Personal health care from a Christian viewpoint, with illustrated exercise section.

Kuntzleman, Charles. *Rating the Exercise.* (New York: William Morrow & Co., 1978.) An extensive analysis of programs and books in the physical fitness field, in conjunction with *Consumers Guide.*

Kunz, Jeffery. *American Medical Association Family Medical Guide.* (New York: Random House, 1982.) A good contemporary medical guide, well illustrated.

Chapter Five

American Medical Association. *Family Medical Guide.* (New York: Random House, 1982.) Helpful discussion on such areas as metabolism, balanced diets, and vitamins.

Amway Corporation. *Nutrition . . . Guide.* (Ada, Michigan: Amway Corporation, 1982.) A study related to vitamin and mineral values.

Brody, Jane. *Jane Brody's Nutrition Book.* (New York: Bantam Books, 1981.) Covers wide range of nutritional topics from caffeine hazards to drinking water. Good health resource.

Chandler, E. Ted, M.D. *How to Have Good Health.* (Nashville: Broadman Press, 1982.) Christian perspective on health. Good chapter on nutrition called "Eating to Live."

Heller, A.L. *Your Body, His Temple.* (Nashville: Thomas Nelson Publishers, 1981.) This is identified as a "balanced Christian view on diet and physical fitness." Well presented material.

Mann, John A. *Secrets of Life Extension.* (New York: Bantam Books, 1980.) Without accepting all of the author's conclusions, you will find this a well-researched volume relating to aging. (Note especially Chapter Six.)

Mayer, Jean. *A Diet for Living.* (New York: Simon and Schuster, 1975.) Dr. Mayer is identified as "America's foremost authority on food and health." He served for a quarter of a century as professor of nutrition at Harvard School of Public Health. The book consists of answers to leading nutrition questions. Helpful appendices.

Pearson, Durk and Shaw, Sandy. *Life Extension.* (New York: Warner Books, 1982.) A current research study on extending the life span through such means as varied chemical input.

Reader's Digest. *Eat Better, Live Better.* (Pleasantville, N.Y.: Reader's Digest Association.) Excellent guide on nutrition and good health. One of the best.

Chapter Six

Havighurst, Robert. *Developmental Tasks.* (New York: David McKay Co., 1952.) The classic study of age-rated developmental tasks.

Kramer, J. J. *The Mobile Home Guide.* (New York: Bobbs-Merrill Co., 1982.) A helpful review of mobile home basics.

Pryor, Hubert. *Your Retirement Housing Guide.* (Long Beach: AARP, 1975.) Housing considerations from an older adult perspective.

Chapter Seven

Adler, Mortimer. *How to Read a Book.* (New York: Simon & Schuster, 1940.) Good example of resources for helping develop an activity.

Retirement Advisors. *Activities: How to Enjoy Leisure.* (New York: Retirement Advisors, 1975.) One of the helpful materials available for older adult planning.

Schaie, K. Warner. *Adult Development and Aging.* (Boston: Little, Brown & Co., 1982.) Chapter eight. Good study on place of activity for older adults.

Tournier, Paul. *Learn to Grow Old.* (New York: Harper & Row, 1971.) Some good reading on older adult concerns, including activity.

Chapter Eight

Dayton, Edward, and Engstrom, Ted. *Strategy for Living.* (Glendale, CA: Regal Books, 1976.) Well laid out and illustrated steps for planning effective living.

Miller, Keith. *The Becomers.* (Waco, TX: Word, 1973.) A personal, practical study on Christian development.

Chapter Nine

Maslow, Abraham. *Motivation and Personality.* (New York: Harper & Row, 1970.) Probably the leading study on human motivation. A classic in the field.

Peale, Norman Vincent. *The Power of Positive Thinking.* (New York: Prentice-Hall, Inc., 1952.) An interesting study of motivational principles by one of America's outstanding clergymen.

Tournier, Paul. *Learn to Grow Old.* (New York: Harper & Row, 1972.) Written from a Christian perspective, this study on the involvements of aging has some good insights on motivation.

Chapter Ten

Dayton, Edward. *Tools for Time Management.* (Grand Rapids: Zondervan, 1983.) A thorough compilation of time-related topics, rich in practical resources.

Engstrom & Mackenzie. *Managing Your Time.* (Grand Rapids: Zondervan, 1967.) Although the book covers the wide area of general management, the first part on Time Management is particularly pertinent for our purpose.

Flynn, Leslie. *How to Save Time in the Ministry.* (Grand Rapids: Baker Book House, 1966.) Although written from a clergyman's perspective, there are many practical suggestions for lay persons.

Lakein, Alan. *How to Get Control of Your Time and Your Life.* (New York: New American Library, 1974.) Written by a time-management consultant, the book seeks to fulfill its title.

Chapter Eleven

Bell, A. Donald. *How to Get Along With People in the Church.* (Grand Rapids: Zondervan, 1960.) A good study on techniques for working effectively with people.

Carnegie, Dale. *How to Win Friends and Influence People.* (New York: Simon and Schuster, 1936.) The premier study on getting along well with people.

Chapter Twelve

Conway, Jim. *Men in Mid-Life Crisis.* (Elgin, IL: Cook, 1978.)

Conway, Sally. *You and Your Husband's Mid-Life Crisis.* (Elgin, IL: Cook, 1980.) Two books on mid-life crisis from a Christian perspective, with helpful material applicable to general marriage concerns.

Gangel, Kenneth. *The Family First.* (Minneapolis: HIS International Service, 1972.) Good analysis of concerns of family in contemporary setting.

Graendorf, Werner (ed.) *Introduction to Biblical Christian Education.*(Chicago: Moody Press, 1981.) Chapters 14 and 15 with bibliographies. Leading textbook in field of Christian education, with good resource unit on family.

Swindoll, Charles R. *Strike the Original Match.* (Portland: Multnomah Press, 1980.) Practical study on Christian marriage, presented in incisive Swindoll style.

Chapter Thirteen

Edman, V. Raymond. *The Delights of Life.* (Wheaton, IL: Van Kampen Press, 1954.) A delightful series of messages and poetry on twenty-eight subjects.

Schaeffer, Edith. *What Is A Family?* (Old Tappan, NJ: Revell, 1975.) The wife of foremost Christian thinker, Francis Schaeffer, and a mother rearing four children at world-renowned L'Abri in Switzerland, Mrs. Schaeffer has compiled a series of helpful observations from her life.

Smith, R. Tilman. *In Favor of Growing Older.* (Scottdale, PA: Herald Press, 1981.) Excellent, practical chapter on "Dying and Death" (11).